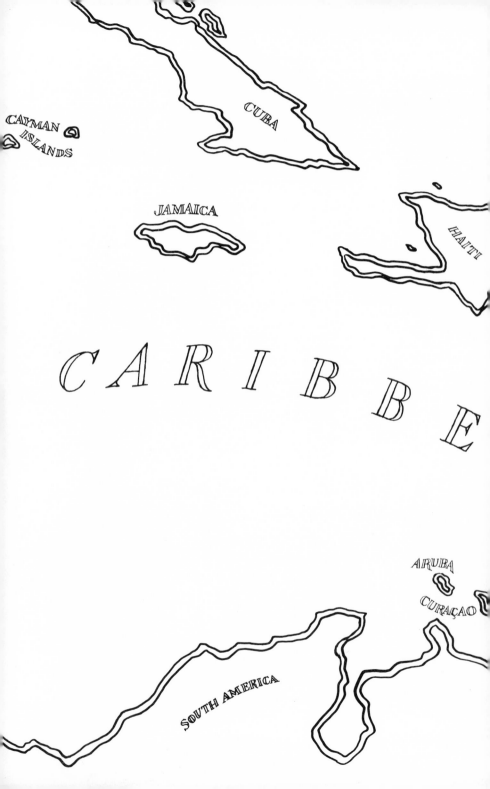

The *Inn* Way...
THE CARIBBEAN

MARGARET ZELLERS

Berkshire Traveller Press
Stockbridge, Massachusetts 01262

THE BERKSHIRE TRAVELLER TRAVEL SHELF

Country Inns and Back Roads 1978, North America
Country Inns and Back Roads, Europe 1978
Country Vacations, USA
New Brunswick Inside Out
Canada's Capital Inside Out
Montreal Inside Out
Great Montreal Walks
The Inn Way . . . Switzerland
The Inn Way . . . Caribbean

Library of Congress #77-20748
ISBN 0-912944-44-7
Copyright 1978 Margaret Zellers
Printed in Dalton, Massachusetts U.S.A. by The Studley Press

COVER PAINTING, BOOK DESIGN, AND DRAWINGS: Janice Lindstrom

Special thanks go to the people of the Caribbean who have taught me so much and have encouraged me to present many of the small places I have found with their help. This book could not have been completed without the enthusiasm, curiosity, and help of my family, Mr. and Mrs. John Zellers, and Sally, Lee, John, and Geoffrey Wallace. Thanks to all of them.

I also appreciate the encouragement of Peter Morgan, Executive Director of the Caribbean Tourism Association, and Minette Lee, Audrey Palmer Hawks, and Loly Martinez in the CTA office, and of John Bell, Executive Director, and Pat Shillito, Executive Secretary, of the Caribbean Hotel Association.

And finally, for his encouragement and understanding sincere thanks go to my publisher and colleague, Norman Simpson.

The inns included in the following pages are those that I know offer a unique holiday opportunity. The choice is based entirely on my own travels to and through the Caribbean, staying at the inns as a paying guest and usually arriving unannounced. There are additional inns in the Caribbean. Future editions of The Inn Way . . . The Caribbean will include them, but these 109 inns I have mentioned will give you some thoughts on how to start traveling the inn way in the Caribbean. Enjoy your travels.

CONTENTS

WHAT IS THE CARIBBEAN?

Carib-BE-an or Ca-RIB-bean, no one seems to know for sure. Even Webster offers both, with Carib-BE-an preferred. There are some who say, "Of course, it's Ca-RIB-bean, for the Carib Indians who settled here," but there are others, trying to be trendy with the new politics, who insist that Carib-BE-an is correct. The British have called it Ca-RIB-bean and "everything British is Colonial and therefore bad." And there are some who prefer one pronunciation or the other "because it sounds better."

No matter what the pronunciation, everyone agrees that the word has two b's and one r, and that the West Indies are the islands that border the Caribbean Sea on the north and east. It's true that Bermuda is far north of the Caribbean (off the coast of Georgia, in fact); and that the Bahamas, and Turks and Caicos Islands, although close to the northern edge of the Sea, are not actually in the Caribbean. The climate in the Bahamas, and Turks and Caicos Islands is similar, but not the same; in Bermuda, winters are cold.

And the West Indies are not the Virgin Islands, although the Virgin Islands are part of the West Indies. The Virgin Islands come in two versions: American (St. Croix, St. John, and St. Thomas) and British (Tortola, Virgin Gorda, Peter Island, and several others). They all splay off in an east-west strip, fringing the Caribbean about 60 miles east of Puerto Rico, on the northeastern border of the Sea.

Confusing? Picture a palm tree planted on the coast of South America at Venezuela and Columbia. Its trunk forms the right-hand "border" of the Caribbean Sea. The fronds, bent to the prevailing trade winds (which blow northeast by east), stretch off to the west, just under the tip of Florida toward the coast of Mexico (and its Caribbean islands of Cancun, Cozumel, and Isla Mujeres).

The lefthand (western) border of the Caribbean Sea is the coast of Central America: from north going south, Mexico, Belize (with its 175-mile reef), a tidbit of Guatemala, Honduras (Roatan Islands), Nicaragua, Costa Rica, and Panama.

The islands in the palm fronds, from west to east, are: Cuba (the largest, 90 miles off the coast of Florida), Jamaica, and the Cayman Islands which, in fact, distort the palm frond image with a huge lump off to the western tip.

Next, heading east, is Hispaniola, the island that is Haiti and the Dominican Republic. Then—as a more traditional clump of fronds—we find Puerto Rico, the Virgin Islands, Anguilla, St. Maarten, Saba, Statia, St. Kitts, Nevis, and Antigua. So much for the palm fronds.

Now for the trunk, sweeping south to the coast of South America: just below Antigua there are, in order, Montserrat, Guadeloupe, Dominica, Martinique, St. Lucia, St. Vincent, and the Grenadine Islands (Bequia, Petit St. Vincent, Palm Island, and others), Grenada, Tobago, and Trinidad. A bulge off to the right (eastern) side, making a triangle with St. Lucia and St. Vincent is Barbados.

The "roots," as we've noted above, are Venezuela (with its Isla Margarita) and Columbia. With some poetic license, we build a house on the coast of Venezuela, west of the trunk, for the islands of Aruba, Bonaire, and Curaçao, a mere 20 miles off the Venezuelan shore.

Got that? O.K. The Caribbean Sea is an area almost 1,700 miles wide by 700 miles long and encompasses such vastly different cultures as U.S.-linked Virgin Islands and South American-oriented Columbia. English-speaking Belize borders Mexico's Caribbean. Barbados, with its British history, is a short plane trip from the French departments of Guadeloupe and Martinique. The ties that bind are often more tightly connected to Europe than to an island a few miles away. The Caribbean versions of the dozen or more cultures imposed on the area by 19th century settlers have developed mostly within each island's own boundaries, isolated for generations by the sea, and with regular communications (via airplanes and airwaves) only within the past 15 years!

For the French, the islands are the "Antilles Française" and the two French island departments are included on a basis equal to those of mainland France: one is Martinique, the other, Guadeloupe with its dependencies of St. Barthelemy, St. Martin, Marie Galante, and Les Saintes.

For the Dutch, "Nederlandse Antillen" refers to the islands of Aruba, Bonaire, and Curaçao in the southern Caribbean, and

Sint Maarten, Saba, and Sint Eustatius, commonly called Statia, in the northern section.

There are the independent countries—Barbados, Jamaica, Columbia, Venezuela, Haiti, Grenada, Trinidad and Tobago among them. And then there are the U.S.-affiliated islands of the Virgins (St. Croix, St. John, St. Thomas) and Puerto Rico; and the British territories of the Cayman Islands, and the Turks and Caicos Islands, a handful of specks sprinkled on the Atlantic off the southeast tip of the Bahamas and just north of Haiti.

Not to be forgotten are the Associated States of England, most of them aspiring to independence, albeit slowly, while they work out the essential financing. These include Antigua, Belize, Dominica, Montserrat, St. Kitts-Nevis, St. Lucia, St. Vincent, and its Grenadines.

The Caribbean is a place where one island with an estimated total of 17,000 visitors last year has an 8,500 foot jet strip perfect for 747 landings—but less than a dozen small hotels. A nearby island that has been receiving a good portion of its annual half-million visitors aboard big jets for years has an inadequate airstrip, now closed for extension and repair.

It is also a place where you can arrive from your hometown aboard a big jet, to make a connection on a 19-passenger DeHavilland Heron, or a smaller plane, where your pilot is the "steward" and the aisle can only be walked if you crook like a question mark.

And, while on the subject of inter-island travel, the Caribbean is a place where you can expect the planes to be small (and late), and you should not wince when the commuter flights have sea spray seeping in around the doors just after takeoff. After all, sea plane is often the fastest service between two seaside towns.

This is a unique part of the world, where pioneering is still a fact of life. It's a place where the sea has been the lifeline for generations, but a lot of the local folk can't swim and wouldn't go near the water in the winter months (when the temperature drops less than 10°) if they could. It's a place where arrivals until a few years ago could only be made by sea—and to get to Bequia and many of the rest of the Grenadines, or to most of the British Virgins and a lot of the other dots, it still is.

Presumably the Caribbean is a place where you go to relax because of the salubrious climate and leisurely pace. And because there is a salubrious climate and leisurely pace, don't count on finger-snapping service—not even when you are paying $90.00 per day.

And don't expect endless water for drinking, even when you are surrounded by it. After all, one of the reasons you are here is because of the "constant sunshine," and because of the constant sunshine, there's seldom rain—and rain is what provides a good portion of the potable water on many islands. The modern salt water conversion plants built to supplement the supply are usually too small by the time they are completed. Construction is slow, but growth is fast.

Put yourself in a vacation mood when you lock the door to your house. Fold your bathing suit into a carry-on case. Be prepared for anything—and for sitting on the beach in the sun while it happens.

The Caribbean is a place where you can don snorkel mask and pluck a local lobster from its rocky crag yourself, but you'll pay $7 US or so to eat a lobster salad lunch at a small island inn. Why? Local fishermen have found that the highrise, chain hotels will pay top dollar for the local langouste (as the lobster is called), so they sell high, even to homefolk who own the small inn up the street.

The Caribbean is a place where you should expect to find small lizards leaping around the place, and you should be prepared for sandflies and other annoying biters just after a rain or in lush, tropical retreats. It's a place where "mountain chicken" is a delicacy (and a local frog); where prehistoric-looking iguanas that used to rule the local terrain and ended up in soups and stews are now preserved wherever they can be found.

Callaloo, fungi, and other local foods almost disappeared in a morass of imported hamburger and steak, but in recent years dasheene, breadfruit, papaya, codfish and ackee, and other local dishes have made a comeback—due, as another example of Caribbean contrasts, to the high duties on imported items to improve local production and keep the cash at home.

The Caribbean is rich in legends which are well worth learning. Tourist Boards and cultural groups have worked to revive fast disappearing songs and dances. Handicrafts, almost rendered obsolete by a local preference for plastic, are being relearned and taught to young people. Foreign artists, drawn by the climate of the Caribbean, have shared their knowledge of silk screen and batik techniques with newly-trained West Indians, and all incorporate Caribbean designs in their work.

The Caribbean is a place where most West Indians saw value in beaches only when outside investors proved their worth— for sunseekers fleeing cold North American winters or drizzly European climes. People from elsewhere were glad to pay money to enjoy a climate West Indians had "for free."

Today the Caribbean is a place where the local residents assert their ownership, reviewing and revising relationships with outside investors and reinforcing the West Indian welcome— a heartfelt one, but now on West Indian terms.

This is an area of emerging nations. It is an area where countries demand the right to make their own decisions—just as the fledgling United States did 200 years ago. And it is an area that will make its mistakes in the full glare of the television lights and near the hand that touches the typewriters.

The Caribbean is an area that too many outsiders fail to take seriously. It is, after all, "paradise" and no one wants problems in paradise.

When you go to the Caribbean be prepared to enjoy yourself. You will. Everyone's trying now. Caribbean tourist officials, both through the Caribbean Tourism Association and the Caribbean Hotel Association, as well as through local schools and organizations, are making every effort to re-establish the traditional West Indian warm welcome.

Government leaders have taken a firm stand on the need to be nice—to each other as well as to visitors. After all, this is an area that has played host to the world from the time of Columbus —to slaves and pirates, to plantation owners and playboys, to sunseekers and to pioneers.

Whatever the Caribbean is, it is not just like home. But, after all, isn't that one of the reasons you want to go there?

CHOOSING YOUR CARIBBEAN INN

Innkeeping does not have a long tradition in the modern Caribbean. Gathering spots that have become inns in Europe and through Turkey may date to the time of the Crusades and before, but when Columbus made his first cruise to the Caribbean in 1492, the islands were inhabited by Indians—the Caribs, a few Arawaks and perhaps some others. Pirateers and other hardy souls followed Columbus's voyages, usually to see what they could pillage and turn into profit.

The Caribbean islands were not known in those days for their hospitality. Visitors were greeted by arrows and bombardments, unless they slipped in stealthily and killed off the original settlers before they were massacred themselves. The huts of the Taino Indians, a tribe of Arawaks, were not hardy enough to survive even the first onslaught, let alone the fires and hurricanes that were to follow.

When settlers survived long enough to start the first communities, most of the buildings were made of wood and thatch which burned quickly, fanned by the trade winds. Plantation owners who came from European countries built huge mansions, often patterned after the best they knew at home; their guests were entertained on the estate so there was no need for inns during that era.

Most of the buildings in which today's inns are housed are new. The oldest of them—some of the original plantation houses—may have a core that dates to the 18th and 19th century sugar days, but it is far more likely that the building in which you stay will have been built in the past ten or twenty years, hopefully in the old tradition but—at least for the inns I have included in this book—with some personality that makes the place special. All the inns I mention have 30 rooms or less.

Since there is no long tradition of Caribbean innkeeping, seldom is a place handed down from father to son or daughter. In fact, offhand, I can't think of one place that has a second generation family tradition as an inn, although some of the owners have a long tradition in the islands. I think especially of the Walwyns who have added flourishes to what was their former plantation house to accommodate guests at Rawlins Plantation in the north quarter of St. Kitts, or Geoffrey Boon whose family had lived on St. Kitts for generations, and who now owns and manages the historic spot called Nisbet Plantation on Nevis, or Mr. Mullings who grew up in Jamaica's Port Antonio and now runs its De Montevin Lodge.

The Hotel 1829 in St. Thomas dates as an inn from that year, but its present owner became an innkeeper less than ten years ago. Casa del Frances on the Puerto Rican island of Vieques was built about 100 years ago by a Frenchman, but its present owners (an American with a French-born wife) bought it about three years ago. Mt. St. Benedict Guest House, in the mountains of Trinidad, was a religious retreat from the time the first shelter was built on the spot in 1911, but the Council of Christian Churches took over the guest house operation a few years ago. The Island Inn near Bridgetown in Barbados became an inn when Allan Martyr opened his home for guests almost 30 years ago, but Martin Donowa, a Barbadian who now runs it, bought it last year.

North American tourism to the islands became a big business about 25 years ago; it dates from the highrise Caribe Hilton's opening near San Juan on Puerto Rico. Today many of the Caribbean people who were first trained in the big hotels are opening their own small inns, acknowledging the need for personality places and attempting to put the personal touch back into travel.

This book is a paean, praising those folk who work harder — and certainly longer hours — than they ever expected to when they took up innkeeping. Their efforts deserve the attention of all of us; their inns provide comfortable nests for those who, like me, would rather have "people" experiences than perfect plumbing and a telephone by the head of the bed.

What to expect:

You can count on cooling trade winds and a warm tropical climate, a crystal clear sea surrounding the island and constant daily sunshine (except when there is "unusual weather"). But you should be aware that there is a Caribbean proclivity for power failures, fresh water shortages, delayed planes, slow service, phones that don't work but sun rays that do. Do not expect—or demand—finger-snapping service. When you do find it, be thankful (if that's what you want); the rest of the time be patient.

Rates: Most of the inns in this book have modest rates, and that means about $35 for two in winter with two meals daily. Rate structures vary from country to country throughout the Caribbean, and so do facilities. For specific rates, inquire from the tourist offices whose addresses and telephone numbers you will find at the end of the introductory comments at the beginning of each section. A handful of places—I think especially of Hotel Castilla at Puerto Plata on the north coast of the Dominican Republic, Marabou in hillside Pétionville above Port au Prince in Haiti, Maison Alexandre on the south coast of Haiti at Jacmel, and the Heron Hotel on St. Vincent—have very low rates, and very simple facilities. A dozen or more places—note Biras Creek and Peter Island in the British Virgin Islands, Arawak Inn on Barbados, Oyster Pond on Sint Maarten, and Petit St. Vincent Resort in the Grenadines—have very high rates, standards, and quality.

Wherever you stay and wherever you go in the Caribbean, it is worth remembering this notice posted and printed by a small inn called Rum Point on Grand Cayman. The following "ten commandments" hint at the humor—and facts—of the Caribbean life:

1. Thou shalt not expect to find things as thou hast them at home, for thou hast left home to find things different.

2. Thou shalt not take anything too seriously, for a carefree mind is the beginning of a fine holiday.

3. Thou shalt not let other guests get on thy nerves, for thou art paying out good money to enjoy thyself.

4. Remember to take only half the clothes thou thinks thou needs—and twice the money.

5. Know at all times where thy passport is, for a person without a passport is a person without a country.

6. Remember that if we had been expected to stay in one place we would have been created with roots.

7. Thou shalt not worry, for he that worrieth hath no pleasure—and few things are ever fatal.

8. When in Rome thou shalt be prepared to do somewhat as the Romans do.

9. Thou shalt not judge the people of a country by the one person who hast given thee trouble.

10. Remember thou art a guest in other lands, and he that treateth his host with respect shall be honored.

Most of the islands included in this book are government members of the Caribbean Tourism Association. Founded in 1951, CTA acts as a catalyst for coordinating the promotion efforts of its members. Organized to provide a forum where members — governments, airlines, cruise lines, and travel agents from the United States mainland — can exchange ideas and discuss areas of mutual concern, CTA has grown to include many business people involved with the Caribbean. Through regular newsletters and frequent meetings, with an annual meeting held in the Caribbean, members have the opportunity to share thoughts on developments in the Caribbean. All are working to assure a comfortable climate for residents and visitors.

The Caribbean Hotel Association has several hundred members among the large and small hotels in the region. Although the primary concerns of CHA are those of its members, the organization coordinates many activities with the Caribbean Tourism Association for greater effect. Membership in CHA is not a criteria for being included in this book, but most of the inns that are mentioned are CHA members, ascribing to the standards of the organization and constantly improving their facilities.

ANTIGUA

One of the first of the Caribbean islands to become a 20th century sun-seekers' haven, Antigua has grown with the times to offer some of the area's most comfortable inns — plus some of the most glorious beaches. The local Tourist Board touts 365 of them. Whether the count is accurate or not doesn't seem to matter as you dig your toes into the strand you've selected.

An English heritage has led to a national passion for cricket, to districts being called parishes, and to each parish having its own English-style church. Modern strides toward independence, from the present status as an Associated State of England, have swept away some of the cane-day British traditions. The country that is evolving is uniquely Antiguan. English is the language, with an Antiguan lilt.

Arriving is easy by cruise ship into St. John's or by air to the airstrip laid by the United States military during the World War II years. BWIA flies nonstop from New York and Miami, Eastern from New York and via San Juan; Air Canada flies from Montreal; and BWIA and Air Canada connect Toronto and Antigua. LIAT, a Caribbean airline owned by governments, makes the connection to the small speck of Barbuda, governed by Antigua and about 28 miles (15-minute flight) to the north.

The star attraction is Nelson's Dockyard at English Harbour restored to look much as it might have when Admiral Horatio Nelson anchored his fleet in the harbor. Yachtsmen of the 20th century put life in the protected cove. For those who want to get an overview there is Clarence House on the hillside across the harbor and open to the public on special occasions. Shirley Heights with its ruins of an old fort is a short drive away. Life in the mid-lands of Antigua is rural, with some cane fields and an expanse of rolling hills, often parched by the strong tropical sun. The capital at St. John's is the place for shopping, both for items of special interest for visitors and for the necessities for everyday life for the Antiguans.

Daytime activity is focused on the sea, on the two hotel-affiliated golf courses and the one public course, and on tennis, with the January Pro-Am Antigua Open Tournament. Sailors gather for the Antigua Race Week, held annually in late April or early May, and can be found around English Harbour where the Nicholson Charter firm is located, at all times. The island market is at its busiest best on Saturday mornings, but will probably be lively enough for most visitors on any weekday morning.

Nightlife is centered on the bigger hotels, or the casino at Castle Harbour, at a place known as Michael's Mount just outside St. John's.

For typical Antiguan style fun, book a room during the August Carnival, a summer frolic with parades, costumes and plenty of calypsos and street dancing. Because it is held in summer, when the pulse of tourism slows, the carnival draws people from many of the nearby islands.

The best beaches are the ones you find for yourself. Sand at all shores is powdery white. The longest strands are at Dickenson Bay and at Jolly Beach. As is the case on most Caribbean islands, all the beaches are public.

For further information, in New York contact Antigua-Barbuda Tourist Board, 610 Fifth Avenue, New York, New York 10020. Telephone: (212) 541-4117. The Antigua Department of Tourism is on High Street, St. John's, Antigua, West Indies (25¢ per half-ounce airmail).

ADMIRAL'S INN, on the shore at English Harbour, about half an hour from the airport and the town of St. Johns.

If I had to select the one inn above all others that gave me the idea for this book a few years ago, this one is it. Admiral's Inn fit my needs at a particular time in my life, and I have always thought of it as my own haven, even when several months pass between visits.

The brand of hospitality I find here is due not only to the nautical Nicholson family (one branch of which kindly lent me a small child to take to a nearby beach for an afternoon of sand-castle building), but also to Ethelyn Philip, who has been the manager since my first visit.

Admiral's Inn has atmosphere. Some of it comes from the fact that it is part of historic English Harbour, Admiral Horatio Nelson's 18th century port. He sailed out from here to military maneuvers and to court Fanny Nisbet, a Caribbean charmer from nearby Nevis whom he met and later married. The flavor of

the harbor is far greater than the sum of its parts; however, if you have a feeling for things nautical, there's the Nicholson charter boat operation, one integral part. And then there's the restoration of the buildings, made of ballast brick joined with molasses-and-sand cement. Even when the inside has been turned into modern apartments (as at the Cooper and Lumber building), the outside is true to tradition. You can wander around in another century with your morning coffee in hand.

There is a handful of shops in the area near the inn. Buy the small booklet (the proceeds go to the Preservation Society of English Harbour) for your guided tour of the restored buildings of Nelson's nest. The nearest beaches are reached by boat. On most of them you can be alone.

The inn, not surprisingly, is a gathering spot for crew and charterers from the many yachts moored here. Darts and conversation contribute to its nautical flavor, helped along by tables on the waterside terrace, and the wood-and-West Indian comfort of a grand old inn.

ADMIRAL'S INN, Box 103, English Harbour, Antigua, West Indies. Telephone: 31027. The 14 rooms vary in shape and size, but all have overhead fans in lieu of air conditioning. Room 1, one flight up, has a big, old canopy bed. Room 7 is my favorite. It's small and up a couple of flights of stairs, but when the window's louvers are opened you can peer through the trees to see the boats bobbing at anchor in the harbor. Other choices include 5 rooms with private patios.

Getting there: Sailing in as Nelson did is certainly a possibility, but most people arrive by rental car or taxi from Antigua's airport, Coolidge Field, about a 30-minute (14 miles) drive across the island.

CALLALOO BEACH HOTEL, on its own white sand beach at Morris Bay, on the sea side of the 37 acres that are part of the estate.
  Management is justifiably proud of the "intimate" hotel that they have created. Although the building is typical of many small hotels that rose on the shores of Caribbean islands in the late 1950s and the early 1960s, the hotel has its own personality that comes in part from the staff and the other guests. There are people who've been coming here for years, and wouldn't go anywhere else on the island, in spite of the vagaries of island power failures and occasional problems with the water pumps.
  The thatched bar area is the pre-dinner gathering place and dining is pleasant in the open-air dining room. Since the entire low-lying complex is within the sound of the swish of the sea, you can be assured of a "typical, tropical inn." Breakfast and dinner are included in your rate here as at most places; if you want a box lunch packed for an island excursion, or if you want to dine on the terrace at lunchtime, you'll pay extra.
  Use of snorkeling equipment or the hotel-owned Sunfish is included in your rate; if you want lessons with either, there's a small charge.
  You can count on a relaxed atmosphere where no one has to fuss a lot about dressing up—as long as you're clean, neat, and presentable.

CALLALOO BEACH HOTEL, Box 676, St. John's, Antigua, West Indies. Telephone: 31054. Guests in the 16 rooms can enjoy a view of the sea and beach from their room. All rooms are twin-bedded, with private bath and shower, and modern fixtures. The high ceilings contribute to the airy feeling of the rooms, which are all alike, motel-style. Floors are tiled, so that sand can be swept out easily and your wet bathing suits won't make a mark. Furnishings are adequate; bedspreads, etc. are colorful.

Getting there: Once you've cleared customs at Antigua's Coolidge Airport, you can take a taxi (for about $10 U.S.) for the 14-mile ride. The capital, St. John's, is about a 10-mile drive from the hotel.

CATAMARAN HOTEL, on the shore at Falmouth Harbour which is the next-door coastline nibble to the famed and historic English Harbour.

The place is nautical, and Hugh and Janet Bailey plan to keep it that way. They are both sailors, and guests who take to the sea will settle in here comfortably, swapping sea stories around the casual, open-air bar.

Catamaran is a comfortably casual kind of spot, appealing to young and carefree types who enjoy tropical living at its natural best. There is some local activity in the village at Falmouth Harbour, but most of the action for guests at the hotel will be what you dream up yourself.

That can include heading around to the next bay (preferably by boat if you can arrange it) to explore Admiral Nelson's dockyard, and to talk to some of the boating types that tie up with their yachts (owned, crewed, or chartered). There's an old fort to poke around on Blake Island, and opportunities for sailing, (both on small boats and on the 30-foot, hotel-owned catamaran, *Sagitoo*). Fishing and snorkeling are included in the rates.

As the Baileys say on their folder, which I had picked up a long time ago and still keep in my files: "There is always a cool breeze blowing in Falmouth Harbour and a warm West Indian welcome awaiting you at the Catamaran Hotel."

True? True!

CATAMARAN HOTEL, Box 958, Falmouth, Antigua, West Indies. Telephone: Antigua 31036. The 11 rooms are simple, but adequate and certainly the price is right. It's low. A couple of rooms have a double bed; others have twin. If you have a preference, state it.

Getting there: The drive from the airport will take you about half hour, and you can count on paying a taxi about $9 U.S. for the ride.

GALLEY BAY SURF CLUB, at a sandy stretch known as Five Islands area, not far from the capital, St. John's.

There's a "small hotel" feeling here, in spite of the size which can put the house count over 50 people when all rooms are filled. Some of the South Seas atmosphere comes from the thatched rondavels that are repeatedly referred to (and now I will also) as "Gauguin-style." The 24 huts that make up the Gauguin Village are a separate complex from the Beach House area, although guests share the same common facilities: beach, pointed-roofed bar and restaurant, and the personality of owner-manager Edee Holbert, when she's on the premises.

There are people who have been coming here for years and think that Galley Bay's calculated, casual atmosphere is just posh enough to make it acceptable. When that crowd is in residence, it can be hard for less-than-gregarious outsiders, unless you enjoy being on the fringes of "someone else's party."

Nothing can distract from the stretch of sand and the calm sea that washes this shore, however. And that is yours to enjoy no matter which rooms you call home. There are riding trails which you can trot around, accompanied by the hotel's recommended horseman, or the tennis court to play a set on. Golf is not far away, and guests can enjoy a day sail in the hotel's 35-foot sloop.

For evening entertainment, if you want more than the moon and the stars, there is dinner—which will take you an hour or two. It can be followed with a local band that plays three times weekly during the winter season; one of those nights is usually on the barbecue night.

The two-mile excursion into the capital of St. John's is an easy outing from here.

GALLEY BAY SURF CLUB, Box 305, St. John's, Antigua, West Indies. Telephone: 20302. The 32 rooms are in the Gauguin Village and in the Beach House, with 24 villas and 8 rooms along the beach. The rondavels are linked, with two for each unit. The bedroom is in one round, thatched hut; the dressing room and bathroom are in the other. Furnishings are rattan to support the Robinson Crusoe atmosphere. The Beach House rooms are typical rectangulars, with pastel-painted walls, private terrace, and simple but adequate furnishings. The beach-and-sea view is the best wall decoration, and it is on the "wall" that leads to the terrace.

Getting there: Antigua's Coolidge Airport is only 5 miles away, but you can count on a $6.50 U.S. taxi fare. The jaunt into town will cost a little less; it is only a two-mile drive.

THE INN, on a hill and beside the beach, across English Harbour from the restoration.

Modern buildings provide all comforts, with a stab at recreating an 18th century atmosphere in the building that sits on top of the hillside. That's where you will find the front desk and the main dining room (with a spectacular view over the sea, the buildings of English Harbour, and the boats lying at anchor in the protected cove.)

A congenial, pub-like atmosphere is suggested by the public rooms at the top of the hill, but when you get down to the beach at Freeman's Bay, where the rooms are located, it's all beach and sea.

Slightly more pristine than the Admiral's Inn across the harbor, The Inn is usually also more "formal" in ambience, if not always in dress. Proper resort attire is de rigeur here during the winter season.

Although most guests loll on the beach or just relax in the cozy beach hut, some prowl the island in rental cars or head into St. John's, the capital, for shopping and sightseeing. The hotel's launch will take you across the harbor to the restoration. Fishing and sailing are easily arranged.

THE INN, Box 187, St. John's, Antigua. Telephone: 31014. The 30 twin-bedded rooms are modern, in two-story units on the beach. All are similar with private bath, patio, or terrace, and the trade winds provide air conditioning.

Getting there: Take a taxi from the airport, about 17 miles away. For sightseeing, you can arrange for a day with a taxi driver or drive around on your own in a rental car.

BARBADOS

Independent from England since November 1966, this 21 mile by 14 mile, pear-shaped island still raises cane (literally). Although Barbados hopes to expand its financial base with hand industries carefully placed in industrial parks around the country, the island's main source of income at present is tourism.

Powdery beaches washed with gentle surf have drawn hotels and hotel guests to the west coast. Some properties are big and well-known, while many are elite and small, quiet resorts that have repeat English, Canadian, and American guests. Rugged surf pounds the east coast. The tradewinds blow from the northeast over the island's historic Sam Lord's Castle, now incorporated in the Marriott Resort, and a host of small, interesting spots. The island's mid-lands are cane fields for most of the year, with hills that rise in the northern section sloping to flatlands at the south coast.

Arriving is easy by air, on BWIA or American to Grantley Adams Airport from New York and Miami or Eastern via San Juan. Ship arrivals are limited to stops at Bridgetown on two-week or longer cruises, and frequent stops by ships based in San Juan and other Caribbean ports.

The star attractions on this island are the Barbadians themselves. Traditional hospitality has survived the pressures of becoming an independent country. The local folk, often called Bajans, delight in sharing their beaches and the pageantry that comes with mid-day musical concerts performed at a seaside gazebo by the uniformed police band. Parades for special celebrations are highlighted by the Barbados Mounted Police.

Action options are focused on daytime, with golf (Sandy Lane and the Barbados Golf and Country Club), tennis at most hotels and at the tennis club outside Bridgetown, scuba and snorkeling arranged through a half-dozen professional firms who divide up the hotel concessions, and a daytime or cocktail cruise aboard the Jolly Roger.

Nightlife is centered on the hotels and a handful of specialty restaurants led, for residents at least, by elegant Alexandra's and gourmet-style La Bonne Auberge. Lively discos lead the action at the big hotels as well as at a couple of spots in Bridgetown and in the heavily-hoteled south coast area.

For typical Bajan style fun (and off-season rates), plan for a vacation in June during the month long Crop-Over Festival. House Tours by the Landmark's Society operate in February and March, and the Garden Club has a special show in June.

Best beaches for peaceful sunning are at coves along the west coast. Busy, action-packed sun spots can be found at the public beach that is a short walk from the Hilton and the Holiday Inn, and at the Marriott's strand of sand on the southeast coast. In the St. Lawrence area, and the rest of the western part of the south coast, there are coves you can share with the fishermen.

For further information contact the Barbados Tourist Board, 800 Second Avenue, New York, New York 10017. Telephone: (212) 986-6516. The Barbados Ministry of Trade External Affairs and Tourism is at Marine House, Hastings, Christ Church Parish, Bridgetown, Barbados, West Indies (25¢ per half-ounce airmail).

ARAWAK INN, at Inch Marlow Point on the south shore of the island.

The "other world' that the Canadian owners have created here is an exotic one. Making the most of the Caribbean's advantages of brilliant sunshine, sea the color of aquamarine, and tropical plants that grow fast and soon cover even the newest buildings with splashes of color, the Arawak Inn looks more Greek than Caribbean.

The inn takes its name from the fact—or legend—that there was an Arawak Indian settlement nearby, in the days before the Caribs took care of the Arawaks, and the British settled Barbados.

The thick white walls that meander around the property define the outline of the place. Within the enclave, brick and cement terraces and pathways are punctuated with small gardens and convenient chairs and tables for leisure time.

Your nest will be in a building that bears a Greek name (Pegasus, Mimosa, Andromeda, Ganymede, and similar names) and will be in one of the clusters of comfortable apartments, each with its own sunning area.

The mingling of the several cultures (Caribbean, Canadian, Greek, and perhaps some Arawak) seems fitting in this place that was built "for the sybarite," as one of the promotion folders proclaims. The newness of it all is refreshing. The surroundings are the ultimate in island luxury and, although the overnight price is high, the atmosphere seems worth it.

The enclave sprouts from a plot of land that runs inland from the shoreline, about ten minutes from Grantley Adams Airport, and about 25 minutes from the metropolis of Bridgetown.

The gathering spot is the restaurant/night club which is at the heart of the area, a few steps from one of the 22 rooms you call home for your visit. An imaginative pool, punctuated with the Mermaid Bar, is at the Caribbean (south) side of the complex, within an easy stroll from your room.

There's a tennis court north of most of the units and a special area between the courts and the pool for sunning, plus the terrace for al fresco dining. This is an elegant, sun-oriented retreat that will appeal to those who are—or want to be with—the "beautiful people."

ARAWAK INN, Inch Marlow, Christ Church Parish, Barbados, West Indies. Telephone: 86101. The 22 rooms are elegantly furnished, in Mediterranean style, making the most of colorful fabric with the white stucco walls. Rooms are named Capella,

Cepheus, Columba, Mira, Mimosa, Pollux, Pegasus, etc.— reminiscent of the Greeks.

Getting there: Fly to Barbados and take a taxi for the 10-minute ride to the inn. The 10-mile ride farther west along the south coast to Bridgetown will take about 25 minutes.

BAGSHOT HOUSE HOTEL, on the coast road at the south, in Christ Church Parish where most of the moderately-priced hotels are located.

The personality for this inn certainly comes from the owner, Eileen Robinson, who opened her very special seaside spot in 1956. She has maintained the old family name for the property, although the construction is new—stucco and boxy. Don't let that description put you off. Bagshot House has plenty of personality, if yours jibes with that of the owner.

The beach stretches out in front of the inn. You can sit in the sun, seaside, all day or you can take one of the public buses that passes nearby to go into town. (You don't need a rental car here unless you want to be on your own for touring all over the island.) There is plenty of activity at the several hotels that are around this inn, but when you are on the grounds of Bagshot you can be blissfully unaware of any of it. If you want to walk outside the gates and down the road, however, you can find a host of diversions, some old and traditional and others new and jumping.

This is a quiet inn tucked into a special spot on the beach. The liveliest entertainment in the evenings is an impromptu party that is "on the house" and is stirred up when Eileen Robinson or some lively guest feels up to it.

BAGSHOT HOUSE HOTEL. St. Lawrence, Christ Church Parish, Barbados, West Indies. Telephone: Barbados 88125. The 16 rooms all have private bath, and neat, tidy, simple furnishings. If you want a room with an ocean view, say so. Not all rooms have that view and the ones that do are special.

Getting there: Take a taxi from the airport to the St. Lawrence area and your driver will find the place easily. It is on the coast road, well before you get to the capital of Bridgetown (which is about a 15-minute drive west, depending on the traffic).

CRANE BEACH, perched on a 60-foot bluff with dunes that sink to the sea where rollers foam in on the shore.

Barbados was one of the first islands I visited when I started traipsing through the Caribbean more than 20 years ago, and Crane Beach was one of the first places I saw. I thought it was spectacular, I had seen nothing like it. I still think it is spectacular; I have traveled the entire Caribbean countless times.

The small inn was the first resort hotel to open in Barbados, according to the present owner, Julian Masters. In 1860, the guests were island planters who vacationed on this shore when they wanted some bracing sea air and a change from the rolling inland terrain. Barbadian families still vacation on this rugged eastern shore, where the sea comes in unbridled. (Continue east and you'll reach Africa.)

What the Masters have done to the Crane Beach Hotel is an example for those who maintain small inns elsewhere in the Caribbean. There's nothing lavish about this place, except spectacular views and its awesome history. The furnishings are simple and, therefore, for me at least, comfortable. White paint keeps the wood looking clean and neat, and the recent addition of a pool just outside the front door, and nearer when you get out of your car than the inn itself, provides a focal point for those who don't want to plunge into the surf from the pink sand beach below.

The food is excellent, partly because the management is smart enough to offer a limited menu, featuring the local lobster and other seafood that can be plucked from the Caribbean. There's a good wine cellar for accompaniment to the leisurely al fresco meals.

There's space on the premises for a couple of shops, and Caribatik, hand-screened fabrics from the Chandler studio near Falmouth on Jamaica's north coast, were featured on one visit. New items are added at the whim of the shopkeepers, but most goods are island-made, a situation I'll do my utmost to encourage.

For sporting types, the Masters can arrange for horseback riding, tennis, and golf, all a short drive from the hotel.

CRANE BEACH HOTEL, St. Philip Parish, Barbados, West Indies. Telephone: Barbados 36220. The dozen or so rooms are marvelous, incorporating the best of their traditional attributes (the wood walls, airy patios, and window views) with the modern conveniences most North Americans insist upon. There are 11 country-style double bedrooms, one studio, one apartment, and four deluxe suites, for a total of 33 beds. The deluxe suites in the south wing have coral stone walls, louvered windows, pinewood floors with island-woven rugs, and antique furnishings. Each has a living room, kitchenette, terrace, balcony or sundeck, and a double bedroom with private bath. If you want to sleep in a four-poster bed, specify when you make your reservations. Not all rooms have them. One of the ground floor suites is known as "Friendly Hall," and one of the first floor suites is called "The Tower."

Getting there: Once you've arrived at the Barbados Airport, hop in a taxi for the 10-minute ride to Crane. You'll find yourself about a 45-minute drive from Bridgetown, the country's capital, but you can easily get there for a day excursion and content yourself with this spot for the rest of your holiday.

ISLAND INN, nestled between two big hotels on Needham's Point, about a 10-minute ride south of Bridgetown.

Many times over the 20 years I have been coming to Barbados, I have settled into the simple surroundings of the Island Inn. The place has not changed much since my first visit, although the surroundings have changed a lot. The Holiday Inn is just behind the small, one-story Island Inn, and the highrise Hilton is a five-minute walk along the road, farther out on the Point. Management has changed a couple of times and I might not have included this inn if not for the present manager, a longtime Caribbean colleague whose innkeeping abilities have earned him accolades at the Caribbean Hotel Association and other area-wide organizations. Martin Donawa became manager at the end of 1977, and opened Brown Sugar Restaurant.

Because Martin is here, you can be assured of excellent food. His Pices Restaurant in the St. Lawrence area has long been island-famous, and he has brought that touch to dining at Island Inn. There's no pool or beach at the hotel, but both are as near as the neighboring Holiday Inn, or the Hilton down the road.

When Allan Martyr ran Island Inn, almost as an extension of his home and certainly with his personality over all, his lore filled the conversational gaps and his love of open air and island simplicity set the tone. Martin Donawa does a similar kind of thing with his own innkeeper's style.

For dining companions at breakfast, and perhaps lunch, in the typically West Indian hotel guests' dining room (which is different from the main dining room for outsiders who make reservations for Martin's special dinners), you will probably find island-wise people on business who pass by this way at regular intervals. The inn is close to the center of Bridgetown, but has all the advantages of a resort.

Island Inn is one of my traditional favorites, but it won't be ideal for everyone.

ISLAND INN, St. Michael Parish, Bridgetown, Barbados, West Indies. Telephone: Bridgetown, Barbados 60057. The 26 rooms are along the hall that leads from the hotel guests' dining room and in the former manager's cottage (4 rooms) at the back of the inn. Do not expect any luxuries, but the basics are there: bed, chair, and a private bathroom. There's great variety in singles and doubles, mostly with regard to size. When you're in your room, you can clearly hear the music from the evening's entertainment as well as a lot of other noises, but they can be comforting. If you're a light sleeper, go elsewhere.

Getting there: When you've cleared customs at the Barbados Airport, take a taxi into Bridgetown. The Island Inn is on a road that turns to the left as you head into town. If you want some exercise, you can walk from the inn into town; otherwise, walk out to the main road and stand on the corner to wait for a public bus.

THE PINK HOUSE, in the northern part of Barbados, on the west coast where the Caribbean Sea is calm.

This very special inn opened in 1958. It was completely refurbished in 1969, and is touched up from time to time, when it needs it, which it did not when I visited recently. Charles Noble and Virginia Noble Lloyd do their utmost to see that you are comfortable in their inn which they operate almost as a private home.

Guests enjoy the fact that there are no special activities, and that the dining room is for their use only, or for their guests whom they may invite after notifying the management so that there are the right number of places set for dinner. You can have (and most do) breakfast in your room, on your own patio.

The beach is a two or three-minute walk from the Pink House, but some guests stay right "at home" for their sunbathing. Appropriate dress, both while sunning and at mealtimes, is the conservative, Caribbean holiday-style that was common throughout the area a few years ago.

Since many of the guests have been coming back year after year, to winter here for ever lengthening stays, there is a "clublike" atmosphere which may get to you if you are traveling alone. On the other hand, if you enjoy casual conversation at sundown, you will usually find congenial conversationalists here.

THE PINK HOUSE, Gibbes, St. Peter Parish, Barbados, West Indies. Telephone: 22403. The 10 rooms are quite varied. They are in four different units; the main house has most of the standard rooms (which are luxury by some standards); there are also a 2-bedroom villa, a 3-bedroom villa and what is known as the Pent House. A patio connects the main house to the villas.

Getting there: It's a long ride from the airport to northern St. Peter Parish (count on at least 45 minutes), but you see most of the island en route. The fare is steep, but the taxi drivers are usually talkative and you can learn a lot. The hotel will send a private car to meet you at the airport if they know your flight number.

SUGAR CANE CLUB, near the northern "end" of the luxury west coast.

A very special inn with the personality of its owner, John

Denton, the Sugar Cane Club gives you all the advantages of having your own home in Barbados. The atmosphere is that of an elegant houseparty. Guests join for the sunset hours, to share conversation about the day's activities which may have been as strenuous as horseback riding or touring the island, or as relaxing as sitting by the hotel's pool or wandering down to the beach, a five-minute walk away.

When Sugar Cane Club opened in the winter of 1970, it was immediately filled with "friends" or friends of friends and that atmosphere has continued since. There's a weekly barbecue with an island floorshow when the house count warrants and otherwise guests can settle into their "own home" to enjoy a quiet holiday.

Clothes for your holiday here should include bathing suits, as well as Riviera-style, casually elegant resort wear. Leave the diamonds at home.

SUGAR CANE CLUB, Maynards, St. Peter Parish, Barbados, West Indies. Telephone: 22261. The 20 rooms vary in size and location since they are in and around a main house. You can count on attractive appointments and the utmost comfort. After you've been here once, you'll have your favorite room for "next year."

Getting there: Take a taxi from the airport and count on a staggering fare and about an hour drive to get across the island and to northern St. Peter Parish.

BRITISH VIRGIN ISLANDS

The several boat-linked British Virgin Islands are scattered in the sea to the northeast of St. Thomas and St. John, the neighboring United States Virgin Islands. Peaceful and quiet — at least since the gold mines worked by 17th century Spaniards ran out and the Dutch, English, and Spanish stopped squabbling over these small specks — the British Virgins are ideal escape hatches for those who like beach-rimmed islands without much action.

The sea is the focus for daily life, and the main route for transportation. Not only do several yacht charter firms keep their fleets based at Road Town on Tortola, but there are motor boats that run "scheduled" services between the most settled of the islands.

Among the better known islands (places where you will find inns for overnighting) are Tortola, with neighboring Beef Island connected by a one-car-wide bridge, and Virgin Gorda, pushed into resort news when Rockefeller financed Little Dix Bay twelve years ago. Others to find for peace and quiet are Peter Island, Marina Cay, Guana Island, and Little Thatch, each with a small inn with the island or cay's name, and Anegada, a flat and sandy island north of Tortola. It's most noted for its offshore reefs and the wrecks of ships that have failed to navigate them. Jost Van Dyke has Foxy's, a sailors' favored restaurant/bar, plus a couple of cottages for rent. Specks like Cooper Island, Carrot Rocks, and Fallen Jerusalem are best known as marks for sailors.

Arriving is the first challenge. Know where you want to go, and be sure that the management at your island base knows when you are coming. They can arrange for the last lap by boat, which is often sent out just for guests. Air BVI flies from San Juan and from St. Croix, connecting with the American Airlines and other flights from mainland U.S. cities. Prinair also flies out of San Juan to the air strip at Beef Island, and charter planes come in when hired. Virgin Gorda's airstrip is used mostly by charter traffic and by Dorado Wings which sends guests from Puerto Rico's Dorado resorts and from St. Thomas. Otherwise, getting to the islands is best by boat, on commercial service out of St. Thomas to West End and to Road Town, Tortola, and by Antilles

Air Boats, the sea plane service that sweeps into the harbour at Road Town on scheduled service from St. Thomas and St. Croix.

Star attractions are the small quiet islands, most of them with sandy coves to call your own. Time has passed these islands by, except insofar as basic comforts are concerned. Hospitality is assured.

Activities will be sea-oriented, and can include chartering a yacht for a day sail or longer. Among the firms operating out of Road Town on Tortola are The Moorings, Caribbean Sailing Yachts (known as CSY) and Tortola Yacht Charters. For scuba diving with the experts, head for Dive B.V.I. operating out of Virgin Gorda's North Sound. Most inns have some link to the sea.

A few places have a tennis court or two, but there's no golf course in the British Virgins. The nearest courses are at Fountain Valley on St. Croix in the United States Virgin Islands, or in Puerto Rico. There are no casinos. Shopping will be limited to a couple of small boutiques if hotel size warrants, the shops in Road Town on Tortola, or at the marina on Virgin Gorda.

Best beaches are those you find for yourself, along the north shore of Tortola, at many coves on Virgin Gorda, the vast sandy strand on uninhabited Sand Cay, or small coves on many of the dots that make up the British Virgin Islands, which you can reach by boat.

For further information contact J. S. Fones at 515 Madison Avenue, New York, New York 10017. Telephone: (212) 371-6755. The British Virgin Islands Tourist Board is at Road Town, Tortola, British Virgin Islands, West Indies. (25¢ postage per half-ounce airmail.)

FORT BURT, on a small hill overlooking the harbor at Road Town, Tortola, B.V.I.

When you settle into one of the chairs on the turret-trimmed terrace at this inn, there's a vast Caribbean panorama before you: boats in the bay, some at anchor, some sailing in or out. Islands on the horizon are a short sail away. Flowers, birds, and the tree frogs that chirp at sunset and the early hours of nightfall provide the special music of the Caribbean.

It was Millie and Chris Hammarsley who founded this place more than 20 years ago when there was little here except the spectacular scenery. The Hammarsleys were special. When luxury, Rockefeller-owned Caneel Bay Resort opened up on

nearby St. John in the late 1950s, guests used to come to Fort Burt
with picnic lunches on day trips. Millie Hammarsley, as one story
goes, packed a picnic lunch herself one day and took it over to
Caneel Bay, to sit in the hotel's fancy lobby and eat it. When told
she couldn't do that, she replied, "Why not? Your guests do the
same every day at my hotel." From that point on a lunch at Fort
Burt, served from the Hammarsley kitchen, was part of the
Tortola trip.

The house that stood on the hill in those days has gone, but
some of the staff who worked at Fort Burt then are still here—
and so are many of the traditions. The place looks different after
the flair and money of Pauline Stewart, a DuPont heiress who
bought and "rebuilt" the place in the late 1960s. The warmth of
the inn in recent years has come from current managers Charley
and Giny Cary, former New Orleans residents who came to the
island in 1969 to operate a flourishing charter boat business
called The Moorings. The Carys now have their own place,
Mariner Inn, at Wickham's Cay II on the other side of town, new
in the winter of 1977-78 during which they managed both.

The handful of guests at Fort Burt dine al fresco, in a center
open-air court behind the main building, or lounge in an inside,
nautically decorated room-with-terrace. There's a small pool
for the use of guests, plus all the many beaches on nearby
British Virgin Islands and cays, as well as limitless sandy stretches
only a 20-minute drive away on the north shore of Tortola. You
can walk into town to find the handful of shops.

FORT BURT, Box 139W, Road Town, Tortola, British Virgin Islands. Telephone: Tortola 42468. For overnight or longer, you have a choice of 7 rooms and 1 cottage, with rooms 1 and 2 just off the dining patio and room 5 up a few steps, overlooking the main building. Rooms 6 and 7 are off to the side, a few steps along the path. All rooms have modern plumbing and facilities and good views of the sea.

Getting there: The taxi from the Antilles Air Boat seaplane dock costs about $1 for the 10-minute ride; from Beef Island Airport, the trip takes about 25 minutes by taxi.

MARINER INN, at the seaside on Wickhams Cay II, reclaimed land in the harbor at Road Town, Tortola.

The two-story units that stretch out toward the sea are built with yachtsmen in mind. The congenial hub is the area in and around the biggest and newest pool on Tortola, with tables nearby for sipping and supping.

Charley and Ginny Cary built this place at the end of 1977 as a headquarters for their charter business, The Moorings, and a place for people to settle in before and after chartering. They also welcome those who like to be where the boating action is. The same warm hospitality that the Carys instilled at Fort Burt now spills down the hill to the Mariner Inn, with Cary-trained staff split between the two properties.

Accommodations here for yachtsmen include everything from showers and chartroom to storage lockers and full maintenance facilities, plus a commissary with full freezer and shelves lined with goods for nibbles ashore or afloat.

All the room furnishings, and as much else as was practicable, were made in Tortola. There's a true West Indian open-air feeling here, in spite of newness, with entertainment (local bands or barbecues) some evenings and congenial nautically-inclined guests and hosts assured all the time.

MARINER INN, Box 139W, Road Town, Tortola, British Virgin Islands. Telephone: 42332. All 24 rooms were new in the winter of 1977-78; all have modern bathroom facilities and a small terrace on both sides of the bedroom/sitting area (the terrace on one side stretches to the neighbor's). Ask for a room on the second floor if you want the best view; on the first if you want to be able to walk out your door and along the waterfront where the boats dock.

Getting there: Take a taxi ($1) from the Antilles Air Boats seaplane dock or you can walk from there if you don't have much luggage; or take the twenty-minute taxi drive from the Beef Island Airport, Tortola's official airport, across the one-car-wide Queen Elizabeth toll bridge.

LONG BAY HOTEL, on a northcoast bay, across the island from Road Town, Tortola and not too far from the town of West End.

When you settle in here, you will be on part of a 50-acre estate, but you probably will go no further than from your room on the hillside on the inland side of the road to the beach which is along the road and the center of daytime activities. The tennis courts get their share of attention from the vacationing doctors and other professional people who have found and love this place.

Long Bay Hotel's attentive staff makes no effort to lure you into joining whatever activities may be in the offing. Your room will have its own sitting area, or at least its own small balcony-with-view, and you can spend all your time there, if you want to.

There is a saltwater pool next to the beach house, just in from the long stretch of white, powdery sand beach with the Caribbean lapping at its shores. If you are ambitious about scuba diving, there are good dive shops operating out of West End and Road Town and the hotel management can make all the arrangements. (They may even have their own connection by the time you get there.)

Other activities—horseback riding, deep sea fishing, and the like—can be arranged if you are patient, but don't count on split second timing or on-the-dot scheduling here. Relax, and enjoy life.

LONG BAY HOTEL, West End, Tortola, British Virgin Islands. Telephone: Tortola 54252. The 35 rooms are either one of the nine suites, which are twin-bedded rooms with shower-bath, a small kitchenette, and a view of the sea, or one of the twelve superior suites which are air-conditioned, with a split-level bedroom/sitting room, as well as a kitchen, bathroom, and balcony, or in one of the seven cottages, each of which have two twin-bedded rooms with tub and shower, plus a kitchen and a living room with view.

Getting there: There are choices for arrival at Tortola, but probably the easiest way is to fly to St. Thomas in the United States Virgin Islands and take the regular boat service to West End, Tortola where you can pick up a taxi to take you for the last stretch, a 10-minute drive to Long Bay. An alternative is to fly to the British Virgin Islands' Beef Island Airport from San Juan, Puerto Rico or from St. Thomas, and then take a taxi for the hour long drive along the south coast, across the island to the north coast to Long Bay.

SUGAR MILL ESTATE, bubbling up the hill from Apple Bay, on the beach-freckled north coast of Tortola.

What happens when a Genesco Corporation executive retires to a remote Caribbean island and has only the leisure life with sun, sand, and sea to occupy his time? He gets bored, and he slides into the hotel business, partly because he has a lot of friends who want to come down and stay for a while. When it opened in the early 1970s, Sugar Mill Estate had only six rooms; more have been added, but the feeling is still "you're a welcome houseguest in my home."

Leonard and Joan Kushins found a 300-year-old sugar mill and decided to buy the plot on which it stood. From that commitment came the kernel for the resort—with the sugar mill being the core of the restaurant which was created when the new rooms were built a couple of years ago. The old walls add atmosphere, but it is the Caribbean which is the spectacular "mural" on one "wall."

There's a botanical garden around the swimming pool, which is up the hill, with the rooms and main house on the inland side of the road. Both the garden and the design of the buildings show the imagination of Joan Kushins, whose eye for color puts the accents on the dining room tables and around the room. Breakfast and dinner are usually served in the Sugar Mill Room; lunch can be served there or by the pool.

Leonard Kushins has been quoted as saying that "the only activities we have are a fresh-water pool and a beach with marvelous snorkeling," but that ignores the opportunities for horseback riding, deep sea fishing, scuba diving, and for sauntering around sleepy Road Town or even sleepier West End before you take off to sail to one of the nearby islets and cays.

There can be as much outdoor activity as you want, but you have to be the innovator. The hospitality comes with your room rate right here on the Estate.

SUGAR MILL ESTATE, Box 425, Tortola, British Virgin Islands. Telephone: Tortola 5-4440. Your selection of rooms, all comfortably (but not lavishly) furnished, includes the four suites that were the original rooms, the twelve studio apartments, and the one honeymoon cottage which gives you a "home of your own." All rooms have kitchen units so you can be completely independent if you want to be.

Getting there: Fly to St. Thomas in the United States Virgin Islands and take the motorboat that operates on scheduled service to West End, Tortola. At West End, you can get a taxi for the 15-minute ride to Apple Bay. You can also take a boat from St. Thomas to Road Town, and take a slightly longer taxi ride from there. A third choice is to fly to the British Virgin Islands' Beef Island Airport from San Juan, Puerto Rico, or St. Thomas and then take an hour long taxi ride to Apple Bay.

SEBASTIANS ON THE BEACH, at Little Apple Bay, a cove on the northwest shore at Long Bay.

The legends of Sebastians thread all the way to St. Thomas where ubiquitous Jerry Sebastian, one of the early escapees to the sun and fun of St. Thomas, had a restaurant/bar on stilts at the waterfront in Charlotte Amalie. That was back in the 1950s, and

Sebastians of St. Thomas was known throughout the islands to sailors and to anyone from the North who knew the Caribbean in those days. Jerry's Sebastians burned down; a new one, without his flair, stands in its place.

Sebastians on Tortola was started by one of Jerry's wives (he had several). Her name was Kay, and when she opened this spot in July 1966, she furnished it with imported china, which you could buy in those days (and did) from any old shop in St. Thomas town, and added a lot of other elegant flourishes. The outpost in the British Virgin Islands was an attempt to recreate a past. It never quite succeeded at that, but it does its own sea-and-sand routine very well.

With those tales told, let's look at what Bill and Eileen Hulse have at Apple Bay today: a pink stucco building on one side of the road that was the original inn, and some rooms on the beach in a two-story, stucco unit that was added as an afterthought and has turned out to offer the prize rooms.

Furnishings are beach-simple, and the atmosphere is oh, so casual. The beach is about all anyone here cares about. The pocket of sand by the building with the rooms is the favored gathering spot for most guests.

SEBASTIANS ON THE BEACH, Box 394, Road Town, Tortola, British Virgin Islands. Telephone: Tortola 54212. Guests in the 15 rooms will either be in the beachside block (12 rooms are upstairs or on the beach level) or in the two or three rooms that are in the main house (and are less expensive). The boxy, new rooms are adequate, but nothing special, unless you have a room with a view of the sea. That makes those rooms spectacular. It is assumed that you will spend a minimum of time inside; all the action is at the beach.

Getting there: Once you've arrived at the British Virgin Islands Airport which is on Beef Island, connected to Tortola by a one-car-wide toll bridge, you'll have about a 45-minute taxi ride to and through Road Town along the south coast heading west before you cross over to get to the northcoast and Long Bay. An alternative is to arrive by the scheduled boat service from St. Thomas in the U.S.V.I. to West End, Tortola, which is a 10-minute drive from the inn. Unless you rent a car, you'll need to arrange with a taxi driver to get where you want to go for the rest of your trip. There's nothing here but Sebastians; Sugar Mill Estate, a possible walk to the east; and Long Bay Inn, a walk to the west.

MARINA CAY, on its own island off the shore of Beef Island.

A gem of a spot that is not as far away as it seems, Marina Cay is a storybook place. It's the main locale for Robb White's "Our Virgin Island," published more than 25 years ago and best tracked down at your local library, unless you're lucky enough to find one of the paperback versions that was issued several years ago.

Even without the book, imagine a speck of an island that rises to a gentle hilltop on which Robb and Rodie White built their home. They eventually turned to innkeeping, to be followed by Allan Batham who ran the place for a while—and

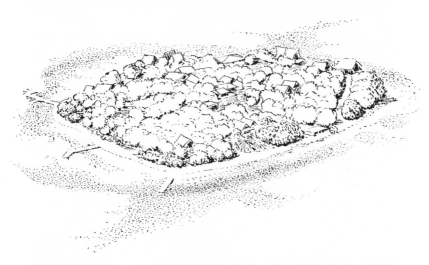

added the crown of A-frames that hold most of the rooms these days. Fran and Mike Giacinto followed as owners and managers, running the place as their home and an inn until their young children were old enough to need better schooling than an isolated island offered.

The focus here is on watersports. Sailors anchor offshore, and make the most of a shoreside, open-air casual café built especially for them and for barbecue evenings enjoyed by guests. There's a scuba shop, with some of the area's best equipment available for rental by guests. Scuba courses are offered, as is sailing instruction, but most of the people who perch at this spot have had some previous experience and are knowledgeable about the ways of the water before they arrive.

The atmosphere is informal. The main house at the top of

the hill is where the dining area is located, open to the breezes and featuring fish and local lobster, sometimes as salads. The living room of the house has become the "indoor" lounging area, with comfortable couches, several books (some left by guests) and island paintings on the stone walls.

Marina Cay is ideal for people who do not want any planned entertainment, and who don't count on anything more dependable than the fact that the sunsets will be spectacular, the surrounding sea is crystal clear, and the sun shines brightly daily.

MARINA CAY, Box 76, Road Town, Tortola, British Virgin Islands. Telephone: 42174. The 16 rooms are in the A-frame cottages that rim a portion of the hilltop, providing guests with a good view out to sea. All accommodations are comfortable, not lavish, with modern plumbing and a sitting area. There's plenty of privacy in your individual cottage; the gathering area for conversation with other guests is at the main house.

Getting there: Fly from Puerto Rico or St. Thomas to Beef Island Airport which is the airport for Tortola (and connected to the island of Tortola by a one-car-wide bridge). Once you get to Beef Island, take a taxi for the very short ride to the pier for the Marina Cay boat — which is often a Boston Whaler. You can walk from the airport if you travel light, and when you stand on the shore, the boatman will see you and speed over to pick you up if he hasn't been advised about your arrival time in advance.

PETER ISLAND, off Tortola, British Virgin Islands.

The cove on which the hotel now stands was once a favorite Sunday haven for friends of mine who lived in St. Thomas. We often headed here by boat, to be the only ones on the island. Not so now.

From the time I sailed around this area in late 1970 and saw huge construction supplies on "my" favorite beach, things have changed. There are only about a thousand acres to the whole island, but some 500 of them caught the eye of Norwegian shipping scion the late Torloff Smedwig who acquired them in 1968. He formed Peter Island Estate-Peder Smedvig Ltd. and began developing, first with the hotel, and then with land plots and houses available for sale to well-heeled buyers.

The property opened in the fall of 1971, with on-the-spot

efforts of a team from Norway led by Thor Greve Loberg and his wife and several other Norwegians, whose job it was to hire and train a staff of British Virgin Islanders. Buildings have risen, with typical island problems, from prefab units sent on Smedvig's ships. Some 20 skilled Norwegians led the work force that put it all together.

Efforts have been made to keep buildings away from the beach; it is about a five-minute walk to get to the choicest

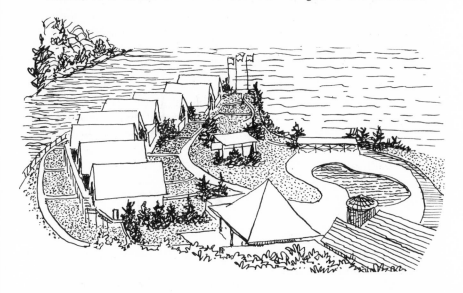

sandy strand. Among the beaches to explore (with a picnic lunch if you wish) are White Bay, Big Reef Bay, and Deadman's Bay — this last the best known and now boasting a small lunch-at-the-beach place that offers simple fare.

There are tennis courts, horses to ride around the island, and plenty of nautical action. Peter Island is definitely sea-oriented and the marina is one of the more luxurious ports for yachtsmen cruising the British Virgin Island waters.

There is a full roster of water activities, including water skiing, fishing, scuba diving, and snorkeling; or you can just sit on the beach. The Peter Island ferry makes several trips daily across the channel (half an hour) to the dock for a short taxi ride into Road Town, the small West Indian capital of the British Virgins with its shops and watering places.

In spite of the luxury tone (and prices), Peter Island is

casual. Here that means the latest in international resort garb. Food is Scandinavian, with emphasis, naturally, on Smorgasbord.

PETER ISLAND, Box 211, Road Town, Tortola, British Virgin Islands. Telephone: 42561. `The 32 rooms are in 8 A-frame cottages, 4 to a unit, with Scandinavian modern decor. Airy and neat, the rooms may seem spartan to some, but all modern conveniences are available and they usually work — a miraculous feat on a small island. You have your own refrigerator, telephone, radio, and television outlet. For those who want their "own" home with utmost luxury, the Smedvig's home, the Crow's Nest, is usually available for rent. The four-bedroom villa is on a hilltop and has all luxuries. Another luxurious house for rent is Sprat Bay House on the beach.

Getting there: A modern, comfortable, enclosed ferry makes regular runs across Sir Francis Drake Channel (which can roll a lot). The trip takes about half an hour and leaves from the CSY Dock which is just before you reach Road Town on the road from Beef Island Airport. Fly to Beef Island, Tortola, via Prinair or other airlines from Puerto Rico or St. Thomas, U.S.V.I.

OLDE YARD INN, not far from the Little Dix Marina and even closer to Handsome Bay.

When Joe and Ellen Devine came to Virgin Gorda and took over this inn, they built a rondavel for their library. The elaborate and extensive collection of good bindings may seem out of place in the tropics when you first look into the comfortable room, but I guarantee that it won't be long before you find yourself curled up there some afternoon with a book, no matter how invitingly the sun beats down outside the arched entryway.

This is a comfortably casual place where the outdoors is the focus of your daily life. Although you can easily walk to most of the bays in this part of the island, there are bicycles to take you farther afield. The inn has a supply of snorkel gear if you've chosen to leave yours home and, if you want a full-fledged authorized scuba course, you can go over to the marina to sign up with the local office for B.V.I. Divers.

There are five trails that weave their way up Gorda Peak and, although most people head to the sea, the flowers and ferns along the trails intrigue those interested in tropical flora. Before you leave the island, be sure to visit the famous "Virgin Gorda Baths," the tumble of gigantic boulders that sequester cool pools of Caribbean Sea in their mass.

The menu for mealtime features fish, and the usual island concoctions are served around the bar. Both the restaurant and bar are popular with yachtsmen, residents, and visitors at other hotels who head here for a night out.

OLDE YARD INN, The Valley, Virgin Gorda, British Virgin Islands. Telephone: Virgin Gorda 55544. The 8 rooms in a separate building next to the main house, face the northeast breeze. They are twin-bedded and have the essentials for comfortable overnighting. There's nothing lavish about the accommodations, but after all, when you book here you should be in search of the simple life with congenial contemporaries.

Getting there: One reason your peace and quiet is assured is because this place is no cinch to get to. There are choices, and all involve several methods of transportation. Probably the easiest route is to charter a small plane at either Puerto Rico's San Juan Airport, or at St. Thomas in the United States Virgin Islands, and fly over to the Virgin Gorda airstrip. From there you can take a taxi to the inn. If you prefer to arrive by sea, there is scheduled motor boat service out of St. Thomas to Road Town, Tortola, and from there you can take a smaller motor boat to come to the Little Dix Marina on Virgin Gorda. When you step ashore, ask someone to drop you off at the Olde Yard Inn, a walkable distance from the marina but hard to find if you're arriving for the first time.

BITTER END YACHT CLUB, on the bay at North South, quiet and remote on Virgin Gorda.

When Robin Lee sailed into the bay about 1966, he stayed on to help Basil Symonette and others build this place. As he reports in his book, *The Dove* (Harper and Row, 1972), "They have found a really lovely spot and they have hauled in all the material they need."

The present owners continue to haul in all the material they need. That includes building materials, foodstuffs (except what comes from the sea), all furnishings, and guests. Only if you come in on your own sailboat (the best way) will you be spared a complex, multi-change arrival route.

Once here, however, you will have found a wonderfully comfortable port. The place is nautical. It calls itself a "unique sailing resort," with use of all the sailing equipment included in your steep daily tariff. You can use the Cal 27 cruising boats, the Rhodes 19 day sailors, the Lasers, Sunfish, and Windsurfers. You can swim at leisure and snorkel offshore, and take scuba lessons in some of the Caribbean's prize waters.

The resort tumbles down to the beach, with the guests housed in hillside villas. Social life centers at the Bitter End Clubhouse for happy hour, mealtimes, and general conversation with the yachtsmen who sail in to anchor offshore.

BITTER END YACHT CLUB, Box 26, Virgin Gorda, British Virgin Islands. Telephone: Virgin Gorda 42746. There are 9 double rooms in the hillside villas. All accommodations are modern, with private bath, comfortable furnishings, and a pleasant patio to sit on to watch the sea and the boats. With a total of 18 guests, and those who sleep on their yachts, the atmosphere resembles that of an elegant houseparty (and, in fact, you and some friends are encouraged to take over the entire place if you can get a group organized).

Getting there: Ready? Sailing is easiest, as I've said. Otherwise, you can fly from Puerto Rico or St. Thomas in a small plane to Virgin Gorda's airport. From there take a taxi to Gun Creek, where, if they know you are coming a small boat will come to pick you up. Boat pickup can also be arranged from the Little Dix Marina on Virgin Gorda, to which you can come by motorboat from Tortola.

BIRAS CREEK, North Sound, Virgin Gorda, British Virgin Islands.

Wrapped like a bracelet on an arm of Virgin Gorda, Biras Creek Resorts, Ltd. is a 150-acre estate that has been developed with taste, its natural beauty preserved as much as possible. The main building caps a hilltop that you see as you approach by sea and that is the only way to approach — either from Gun Creek dock or from the mooring where you've left your yacht.

There's a swimming pool for those who don't want to go further than a step outside the cottage door, but the real beach is a short walk to Deep Bay where a beach bar usually offers some low-key activity.

The main house is the gathering place at noon and dusk. In addition to bar and dining room with view, there's a small shop with emergency rations (suntan oil, hats, beach cover-ups, and a few island-made items).

But getting here is the real challenge. Speedy is the entrepreneur of this island. If you haven't come over from Road Town, Tortola, on his motor boat to Little Dix Marina, you're sure to meet up with him, or one of his drivers, in a car when you tackle the land portion of this jaunt. Brace yourself for an up, over, and around bouncy route on a mostly unpaved road, for almost an hour's ride, to the Gun Creek dock.

There are some small villages along the way, but it's the offshore scenery that is truly spectacular. The plunge from a small settlement to Gun Creek dock seems to head straight into the sea. When you stand on the dock, the boat soon appears and you can speed to the Biras Creek dock in five minutes, salt spray flying in your face. This is not a route for spiffy clothes and lots of luggage. Travel light and comfortably.

Once there, all is luxury—and lively, when the other guests are. Dress is casual chic, with plenty of suntan showing.

BIRAS CREEK, Box 54, Virgin Gorda, British Virgin Islands. Telephone: 55525. The secluded luxury of the 15 units, each with two suites, on a cove along the shore, is ideal for those who want peace and quiet. Suites have a bedroom and divan beds in a sitting room, plus private bath, and a patio. Refrigerators are in all rooms. The main house is a short walk up the hill; tennis courts are a stroll past (or through) the bird sanctuary-lagoon nature area. Boats rock gently at anchor in the bay.

Getting there: The outpost ambience is assured by the fact that, although the hotel is at the end of a peninsula on North Sound, there's no road to it. Sailing in is best, but failing that, fly to St. Thomas, U.S.V.I. or San Juan, Puerto Rico for small plane service to Virgin Gorda. From the simple airstrip there, take a taxi to Gun Creek dock for the boat (usually a Boston Whaler) to Biras Creek. Another route, if you've planned ahead, is to arrive at the Little Dix Marina by boat or plane-and-taxi, and have the big boat pick you up for the trip up the coast to North Sound and the hotel.

CAYMAN ISLANDS

Still a British colony and proud of it, the three Cayman Islands quietly go about the business of banking and building quality small hotels and condominiums for visitors who want to bask in the sun. The three islands are less than 200 miles south of Cuba, and about 150 miles northwest of Jamaica. Prior to Jamaica's independence in 1962, the Caymans were ruled by England through Jamaica. Links are still strong, with daily flights between Jamaica and Grand Cayman and Jamaica-made items for sale in Caymanian shops. Politically the two areas are worlds apart.

Since 1966, the Cayman Islands have posted their future on providing offshore banking facilities and creating a tax haven. A crop of banks thrives in the new buildings in the capital, Georgetown. While Grand Cayman, the biggest of the three islands and the seat of the government, offers the most complete program of activities, salt water sportsmen enjoy the rustic and remote facilities offered on Cayman Brac and on even smaller Little Cayman where the exclusive Southern Cross Club is the only place to stay.

Arriving in the Caymans is easy, via an hour-long flight from Miami (over Cuba) to Owen Roberts Airport on Grand Cayman. Cayman Airways connects Grand Cayman and the two smaller islands, as well as making the link to Jamaica. LACSA and Southern Airways also fly to Grand Cayman from Miami.

Star attractions on the Caymans are water-related. Underwater enthusiasts searched the reefs offshore long before scuba became so fashionable. Today the Caymans lead the list of places for that sport. Professional training for scuba certification is offered through several expert firms. Snorkeling can be enjoyed by beginners as well as those who have searched the offshore reefs of other Caribbean islands.

Action options include a burgeoning tennis community as well as all the watersports (scuba, waterskiing, snorkeling, sailing, swimming). But if you must have golf—for the moment you'll have to go elsewhere. There's no golf course here.

Nightlife is led by the disco called the Wreck of the Ten Sails at the Grand Caymanian. Other options are dining out, perhaps to the tune of some local band, or sitting around listening to the songs of the Barefoot Man. Evening cruises are offered by some of the watersports firms, and night diving is popular with expert scuba divers.

Best beaches are those on Grand Cayman, and the strand locally known as "Seven Mile Beach" at West Bay is the Caribbean's best beach. You can walk for more than four miles along the entire strand, passing most of the island's hotels on the way. There are smaller beaches elsewhere on Grand Cayman, as well as on Cayman Brac and Little Cayman.

For further information, Cayman Islands Tourist Office has a representative at 420 Lexington Avenue, New York, New York 10017. Telephone: (212) 682-5582. On Grand Cayman, the main office is the Department of Tourism, Box 67, Georgetown, Grand Cayman, British West Indies. (25¢ postage per half-ounce airmail.)

BUCCANEER'S INN, 2 minutes from the airstrip on the island of Cayman Brac, off the shore of Grand Cayman.

"Cayman Brac is for romantics," according to Glorine Scott, manager of this inn, but it is also for people who like their sun and sea pure, without a lot of modern trappings. More like a camp than a resort hotel, the inn provides all the basic comforts, but counts on its guests to be self-sufficient insofar as prowling around the island for caves or birdwatching or heading out to sea for fishing. You can stand in the shallow flats for bone fishing, taking your cue from your guide who will probably use minnows for bait (and will toss the fish back in after the day's sport is over).

You can also choose an all-day fishing excursion off Little Cayman, the third of the Cayman Islands; the hotel will pack your picnic lunch.

The inn was a private residence for the first part of its history. Anton Foster built it and lived here until the romance that inspired him to build the two-bedroom, two-bathroom house dissolved with the departure of his fiancee. His father, Captain Bertie, then took over to use the house for guests. The Scott brothers, grandsons of Captain Bertie, bought the property in 1973 and have refitted and refurbished, but haven't changed the original personality of the first inn which opened for guests on December 3, 1955.

You're respectfully requested not to wear jacket and tie or to dress up; but otherwise you can wear whatever you will. Anything comfortable is usual evening wear, with bathing suits the uniform during the day.

The menu often features fish, since most other items must be imported from the States via Grand Cayman. Count on congenial conversation as your dinner entertainment unless the small island band performs.

On the premises you will find a saltwater pool, a completely equipped Dive Shop, a couple of duty-free shops with limited selection of merchandise, and some second-hand paperback books to read if you haven't brought your own.

BUCCANEER'S INN, Box 68, Cayman Brac, Cayman Islands, British West Indies. Telephone: 87257. The 24 rooms have modern appointments, with the ten added in 1976 referred to as the "deluxe" rooms. These have two double beds, wall-to-wall carpeting, private bath and shower, and a screened-in porch. You will need the screens (and your favorite gnat and mosquito repellent) for twilight — and sometimes daylight — comfort. The other eight standard rooms have private bath, two single beds, and a patio. Furnishings are not opulent, but they are comfortable.

Getting there: Allow plenty of time and relax. Once you arrive on Grand Cayman, you'll have to change to the small plane for Cayman Brac. "Schedules" often mean that you have quite a wait, so give some thought to booking a room on Grand Cayman and flying over the next day. Once you arrive on Cayman Brac, you are practically at the inn. If they know you are coming, they will be at the airstrip when the plane arrives. If not, don't worry, there will always be a ride.

RUM POINT, at the tip of a peninsula that juts into the sea, in the middle of the north coast of Grand Cayman.
When Bruce and Doris Parker first found Rum Point several years ago, at the end of a one-car-wide rutted path, the time was during days of escaping to the Caribbean. The Parkers had been living in the Bahamas (Bruce was a National and World Champion waterskier and held the record for waterskiing from Nassau to Miami), but they were searching for their own paradise in the sun. They bought Rum Point Club and turned it into a true tropical Eden. They have raised five children, a couple of parrots, and a dog, Sir Rummy Motley, during the ensuing years.

Tahiti comes immediately to mind, if thoughts of Robinson Crusoe haven't already filled your head. Rum Point is casual — barefoot casual — and perhaps that's too casual for some. The same atmosphere that can make you abandon all cares and relax easily in the thatched beachside area has also resulted in a relaxed management that gets things done when the spirit is willing.

If you want a spectacular beach, a typical, tropical lounge, and an emphasis on water sports, then Rum Point might be ideal. If you expect lots of service and housekeeping that could endure the white glove treatment, choose another place. No one here worries about the sand you track into the room. If it bothers you, then it's up to you to do something about it yourself.

Bring some books, ask about the inn's eclectic collection, or be happy with conversation as the main entertainment, besides what you find in and on the sea. Fishermen beach their boats near here and discussing nautical lore with them can be the biggest diversion of the day.

The food in the comfortable dining area includes recipes prepared from the cookbook that Doris Parker has for sale (with a wood cover and a high price). Specialties while you are here (even if only for lunch or dinner while you bed somewhere else) could include conchburgers or conch fritters, shark steaks, turtle fondue, sea horse gumbo — or trout!

You will feel no pressure as you wander along the stretch of powdery sand outside the doors of the inn or swim in the Caribbean that laps at the shore. A quiet retreat, Rum Point is for those who search for sun and sand and serenity without frills.

The hotel provides full diving facilities (tanks and all equipment included in dive cost for experienced divers), plus half-day snorkeling trips and an underwater photography course. Fishing can be arranged for about $60 for from one to four people and waterskiing is possible too.

RUM POINT, Box 510, Grand Cayman, British West Indies. Telephone: 7-2535. The 10 rooms are very informal, on two levels of an arm off the main building. Shower/bath facilities are there, but not lavish. This is the casual tropics.

Getting there: The taxi ride from Owen Roberts Airport will take you about an hour and will cost $22.50 U.S. The same cost applies for the run to Georgetown, the capital, about the same distance from Rum Point as the airport. (At that price, renting a car for a couple of days is worth it if you want mobility.)

TORTUGA CLUB, at the east end of Grand Cayman, near Rogers Wreck Point.

When Eric and Suzy Bergstrom chose this east end point as their home, the place was near some of the island's best scuba and snorkeling sites, but a long way from anywhere they had known in the United States or even on Grand Cayman. For most people who arrive here today, it is still a long way off — especially from the airport and from Georgetown, the main town on Grand Cayman. It takes about 45 minutes to drive out. The roads are better than they used to be, but even so, once here you won't want to leave, except to plunge into the sea. The Bergstroms opened Tortuga Club in 1958, and have raised their family of five here. They sold the place to people from California in early 1978, but the crop of devoted visitors still come back from season to season, to find again the seaside pleasures that never fail to provide a peaceful vacation.

When you recall that Tortuga means turtle, it is not surprising to see turtle shells as decor on the walls and elsewhere. Roofing is thatch, at least at the beach pavilion, where several hammocks are tied to the center of the pole, leaving you free to spoke out to the other post, head first or feet first.

Ping pong is available, but most people head straight for the sea. There's a choice of waterskiing, Sunfish sailboats, and scuba lessons (with resort and certifications courses offered), and an opportunity for deep sea fishing if you make your interest known.

Shopping time will be spent in Georgetown. You can probably ride in with one of the other guests when they go into town if you haven't rented a car. Unless you plan on a lot of touring, you won't need one.

TORTUGA CLUB, Box 496, East End, Grand Cayman, British West Indies. Telephone: 7-2488. The 14 rooms are in a wing along the beach, motel style, with simple but adequate furnishings, a doorway out to the shore, and coffee served in your rooms — at your bidding.

Getting there: If you let the management know when you are arriving, arrangements will be made to have a taxi driver meet you for the almost-an-hour-long ride to the Tortuga Club. Otherwise, hail your own cab (if one hasn't already hailed you) and expect to pay $22.50 for the ride from Owen Roberts Airport.

DOMINICA

Unique in the Caribbean, with its jungle, its Carib Indian Reservation, and its island-wide tangle of tropical growth that turns the entire 30 by 15 miles into a botanical garden, Dominica is relatively unknown to the outside world. Its role in history has been as a pawn in power plays between the British and French, the British claiming the "decisive" victory in the 19th century when the island came firmly under British rule.

Located between two of the largest French West Indies, Guadeloupe and Martinique, Dominica's language and customs reflect patterns that are obvious in the French islands. Island rule in recent years has been as an Associated State, with strides toward independence from England as soon as the essential financing can be worked out.

Arriving on Dominica is easiest by air, from the neighboring French islands or on island-hopping flights from Barbados or Antigua. Day excursions are offered from both Martinique and Guadeloupe, but Dominica deserves more time. Yachtsmen cruise in, usually to the town of Plymouth on the northwest coast (where the harbor is better than that at the capital of Roseau).

Star attractions here are the natural tropical growth (some portions of the tangled interior have never been explored), the reservation where pure-bred Caribs are the last remaining community of the Caribbean's earliest settlers, and the many waterfalls that splash into pools that offer some of the island's best bathing.

Action options are related to nature. The Armours, owners of one of the island's inns, operate several tours of the interior. Some excursions are by jeep to visit waterfalls, the National Park, and the Carib reservation; other options are river journeys in dugout canoes or fishing outings offshore. There are no golf courses or tennis courts on Dominica.

Nightlife is limited to listening to the jungle noises, or to an occasional performance by an island musical group. When there are festivities in Roseau, it may be worth making the journey into town — depending on where you've chosen to overnight.

Best beaches are at the northeast coast, and not near any of the hotels. This is not an island to head for if beaches are your prime Caribbean concern.

For further information, contact the Caribbean Tourism Association, 20 East 46th Street, New York, New York 10017. Telephone: (212) 682-0435. On Dominica, the Tourist Board is reached through Box 73, Roseau, Dominica, West Indies. (25¢ postage per half-ounce airmail.)

ANCHORAGE HOTEL, on shore, a mile or so outside the town of Roseau, in the south of Dominica, W.I.

To get here you have to be prepared to spend at least two hours bouncing over and winding through some of the Caribbean's most majestic scenery: mountains, waterfalls, thick shining banana leaves, lime trees, bursts of flowers, and the area around Sinicou, the only Carib Indian reservation and a place where you can stop to talk and watch the Caribs work on gommier canoes, carved from long, straight tree trunks.

The trip is well worth the effort it takes. When you arrive you'll find a special place on this unique island. The Armours, owners of the Anchorage, are experts on Dominica and operate several jeep and boat tours that prove it. You will never wonder what to do next (although you can always do nothing if you want to); they will tell you as much as you want to know about their unusual island.

The hotel is their home, with a three-story unit overlooking its shoreside pool and additional rooms on what used to be the tennis court, along the water on the other side of the main building. Food is strictly Dominican, partly because of government imposed customs regulations, and partly because Janice and Carl Armour know and share good Dominican cooking.

In addition to the small town of Roseau (the island's biggest and its capital), with shops and a couple of small restaurants, there's the whole verdant island to explore. Tennis is hard to find now that the new units have taken over space once allotted to the courts. Landlocked sailors will enjoy talking with those who anchor offshore, using marina facilities prepared by the Armours.

ANCHORAGE HOTEL, Box 34, Roseau, Dominica, West Indies. Telephone: Dominica 2638. Guests in the 30 rooms will have modern but not lavish conveniences, with sea views from most rooms and balconies or patios on all. Air conditioners are available, but the salty sea breeze is best.

Getting there: I've already mentioned the jouncing, bouncing ride so there's no need to go over that again. Just be ready for it to be as bad as possible, and then you'll be pleasantly surprised. Taxi fares are rapidly rising. If you make your reservation far enough in advance, the Armours will arrange to have a driver meet you.

FORT YOUNG, in the heart of Roseau, a two-hour drive southwest from the airport.

This is the traditional spot to stay and, until the Armours added to their home to create their very special Anchorage Hotel, Fort Young hosted all the business travelers and anyone else who wanted to be in the center of Roseau.

The old fort is hardly recognizable, although an early brochure claims that it is the governing factor for the hotel. You will enter through a boxy fortress that claims to be the 18th century fort, and once inside you will have all the advantages of the modernization that includes air-conditioning (in some rooms, not all), a swimming pool and a restaurant. These last two are the hub of activity, not only for guests, but for many of the townsfolk who seek out this spot for lunch, dinner or a respite from the workaday world.

One of the brochures from the hotel claims that "by combining the old stone buildings of an 18th century fort with entirely modern kitchen and bedroom wings, an atmosphere of unusual distinction has been created. History of the past is blended with the needs of the present."

In the roster of island hotels, what is "entirely modern" in Dominica may seem strictly '50s and nothing special, but the location is ideal for those who want to be within walking distance of capital sights.

FORT YOUNG HOTEL, Box 8, Roseau, Dominica, West Indies. Telephone: 2251-3. There's a lot of variety in the 26 doubles that fill a half-moon shaped building around the pool. Some are air-conditioned; those with a lower price are not. If you pay for the best accommodations in the house, you will be in an air-conditioned room with private bath, balcony, and easy access to the swimming pool.

Getting there: Once again I say brace yourself for the 2-hour bump-and-rattle ride from the airport, a strip of runway on the northeast coast, to Roseau on the southwest shore. One advantage of this inn is, however, that you can walk to anything you will want to see or do in town, and can therefore avoid the bump-and-rattle car ride most of the time.

ISLAND HOUSE, in the mountains about a 20-minute drive (5 miles) up and out from seaside Roseau.

When Margie and Pete Brand opened this place in the 1960s, this was to be the perfect tropical retreat, tucked into the lush foliage overlooking the Caribbean Sea. It has never been a haven for the beach crowd (the nearest beach is black volcanic sand, and a bouncy drive away from the inn), but has always lured self-sufficient, independent types, often professional people in search of a quiet, tropical spot where jungle walks and the nearby village of Wotten Waven are some of the entertainment options.

The inn's buildings have been designed to make the best use of the local wood and stone, with the result providing a tropical retreat that is ideal for the modern Robinson Crusoes who want just a little bit more luxury than Crusoe and his man Friday knew. You will have your man Friday assigned to you by the hotel management for the duration of your visit. Although the original system has slackened some in recent seasons, there is still a policy of one staff member for each guest and it is *your* staff-guide who will answer all your questions, see that meals are delivered to your room if that's what you want, and generally over see your stay.

The place you call home will be one of the handful of cottages that cluster at the spring-fed pool. The mountain air and Dominica's unique climate assure the fact that this spot will be cooler than most tropical retreats. Bring a sweater. As the Brands admitted in an early folder about their special spot. "All our days are warm but they are not hot," but "you can sunburn at our poolside in only a few minutes if you are incautious."

The hub of hospitality is the main building with its fireplace, with its welcomed warmth on cool evenings.

When things are going full tilt at this unusual Caribbean inn, you can enjoy special Sunday barbecues, sometimes with suckling pig; wine with dinner; fresh baked breads (including banana bread); and special island foods such as the local crayfish and crapaud or "mountain chicken" which is the local frog.

Daytime activities are centered on nature: walks along paths through verdant tropical growth; bird-watching; hiking to some of the island's many waterfalls; perhaps a dunk in the pools of waterfalls or a visit to Roses Lime Juice factory or the Dominican Convent where sisal rugs are woven in Roseau; a river cruise in island-carved dugout canoes or a visit to the Carib Indian Reservation. You can do your touring on a guided jeep-safari, or on your own in a rental jeep if you are up to disciplining the car over the pot-holed and disappearing roads.

Count on other guests, a good book, or a lot of sleep for your evening activities. After dinner, the place collapses.

ISLAND HOUSE, Dominica, West Indies. Telephone: 2817. The 18 double rooms are in several units, each different from the others and 10 of them with tub and shower. The remaining 8 have shower only. All the units have personality, with A-frame thatched roofs and porches for leisure time spent amidst the verdant growth.

Getting there: Fly to Dominica from the nearby French islands of Martinique or Guadeloupe, or via Antigua on LIAT. Then brace yourself for the almost 2-hour drive on rutted roads. Once you arrive at Island House, you will be about a 20-minute drive (4 and 3/10 miles) from the island capital of Roseau.

RIVIÈRE LA CROIX ESTATE HOTEL, inland, almost an hour drive up into the hills above the shoreside capital of Roseau.

If your idea of an island retreat includes jungle, consider this outpost. Built a few years ago and favored by botanists and others who like to be surrounded by tropical flora and fauna, the seven cabins are sprinkled among lush growth, with connecting pathways providing the link with your neighbor and with the central buildings.

The perch is about 1600 feet high, on a 50-acre estate that is a working plantation of grapefruit, limes, oranges, bananas, coffee, and the other products that thrive on Dominica's verdant mountainsides.

The main building, built of wood and trimmed with bougainvillea and other bright blooms, is the center of the hotel's activities, with the pool a drawing card during daytime hours. The estate is a popular place for the luncheon stop of day tours from nearby Guadeloupe and Martinique. If you've headed to this spot for peace and quiet, you may find that tour days are the time for you to head into the hinterlands, to visit the Carib Indian Reservation, to take a walk to the nearby river for your swimming or to go offshore for a day of fishing.

Evening hours are quiet, with dinner by candlelight in the main dining room or buffet style by the pool; the jungle noises are the "musical entertainment" for most evenings.

Those who knew of this place when Bill and Biba Ure were the resident hosts will miss their unique brand of hospitality. Dr. Klaus, the present owner, is on premises a lot of the time and, in his absence, things seem to run smoothly, if somewhat more independently. Rivière La Croix is for self-sufficient types who like to live in the woods.

RIVIÈRE LA CROIX ESTATE HOTEL, Box 100, Roseau, Dominica, West Indies. Telephone: 1354. The 7 cabins are near each other, but assure privacy for those who settle into the simple wood structures which are built on stilts so that they do not slant to the hillside. The central building has a pool and is the hub of the action. All rooms have a porch area, with a twin-bedded main room behind it and the bathroom/dressing room at the back.

Getting there: Once you've landed at Dominica's airport, you'll have a long and bumpy ride to the 50-acre estate. Plan on about 1½ hours. The ride from the hotel to shoreside Roseau will take about 45 minutes.

CASTAWAYS HOTEL, on its own black sand beach about 13 miles north of Roseau.

Some friends of mine can survive the rigors of working in New York only because they know there is a place like Castaways that they can head to when the commercial pressures get to them. Fortunately for some of us, Castaways' time as one of the inns affiliated with the Club Caribbee attempt at a pseudo-Club Med, swinging, all-inclusive-priced holiday was short-lived. Castaways has reverted to doing what it has always done well: providing peace and quiet in comfortable, tropical surroundings on one of the Caribbean's most unusual islands.

Dominica is different. Most of the island is a tropical jungle and the roads are deplorable. There's no better word for them.

They are rutted and, after the heavy rains, often washed out, but that seems to support the outpost atmosphere that those who find this place enjoy.

On an island with very few beaches (and none that are spectacular), the fact that Castaways gives you an enchanting volcanic sand strand to sink your footprints into is a definite plus.

There's not a lot of planned action here. You can enjoy some unusual diversions such as visiting the Carib Indian Reservation, going to the waterfalls and through the verdant countryside on bird and flower walks or heading into the Dominican capital of Roseau for market day. Otherwise, you can spend your daylight hours in, on, or under the sea, or lolling on the beach, book in hand.

CASTAWAYS HOTEL, Box 5, Mero, Dominica, West Indies. Telephone: 6244. The 28 rooms are modern, motel-style with comfortable furnishings and colorful fabrics. Most rooms have a balcony/terrace arrangement and island-woven rugs on the wood floors. This is an informal place for outdoors-oriented people who want a quiet retreat.

Getting there: First fly to Antigua and then to Dominica, unless you fly over from Guadeloupe to the north or Martinique to the south. (There are special excursions from both the French islands to this unusual British-affiliated island.) Once you arrive at the airport, brace yourself for the rutted and rugged 2-hour drive to Castaways, some 20 wiggly miles from the airport.

DOMINICAN REPUBLIC

An independent country with a vibrant Spanish culture, the country claims the oldest European city in the New World. Its capital of Santo Domingo was the home for the Columbus family. Christopher is buried in the cathedral; his brother, Bartolomé, lived here briefly; and his son, Diego, was the ruler of the Spanish colony when he lived at the Alcazar with his wife.

The country occupies the eastern two-thirds of the island of Hispaniola; Haiti covers the western one-third. Agriculture has been, and is, the main source of income, with sugar the leading crop, and nickel and other natural resources high on the list of island exports. Tourism came to the attention of President Joaquim Balaguer as a labor intensive industry and some of the contributions that the Dominican Republic has made to the Caribbean's resort roster are the area's most luxurious.

This is not a country for small inns. The places that do exist in the towns around the country are often too rustic to be comfortable for visitors who expect modern conveniences. The one exception—and an inn that I hope will spark an enthusiasm for personality places to stay around this exceptional country— is the place I discovered in Puerto Plata, the Hotel Castilla mentioned below.

Arriving at Las Americas Airport can be nonstop on American Airlines or Dominicana from New York, or Dominicana from Miami. Prinair, Eastern Airlines and others fly from San Juan, Puerto Rico. Small planes of Alas del Caribe fly to towns around the Dominican Republic from Herrera Airport, about five minutes from downtown Santo Domingo. Ships head south from Miami to Puerto Plata, a city on the north coast, and into the new pier at Santo Domingo, on the south coast.

Star attractions for this country have a Spanish flavor. For those who like elegant (and expensive) restaurants, Santo Domingo has an international roster of exceptional places. Casinos and "quicky divorce" laws lure some visitors, but most head for the tennis and golf available at the Costasur properties at the town of La Romana. Those who stay near the city should spend a couple of hours with the history of downtown Santo Domingo's restored area. Spanish is the language of the country; don't count on fluent English, except at big hotels and even then be prepared to speak precisely.

Action options in the capital include the casinos and nightclubs, the cultural center and the shops and cafés of the area known as Atarazana around Diego Columbus' former home. Resort life centers at La Romana, mentioned above.

Best beaches are along the north (and windy)coast, stretching out from Puerto Plata east toward Sosua and other towns. There are small coves near La Romana, and white powdery sand rims the beach at Catalina Island off the shore at La Romana. Beaches are not the number one reason to head to the Dominican Republic.

For further information in the United States, contact the Dominican Tourist Information Center, 485 Madison Avenue, New York, New York 10017. Telephone: (212) 826-0750. In the Dominican Republic, there are offices in Santo Domingo, near the cathedral.

HOTEL CASTILLA, in the heart of the north coast town of Puerto Plata.

I strolled through the doorways of this hotel on a recent visit to Puerto Plata, little suspecting that I would find a Sydney Greenstreet retreat inside. Imagination and the eye of a creative decorator from New York have turned this simple corner hotel into a gem.

Don't expect all modern conveniences. There are plans to spruce up the rooms, but the upstairs accommodations I saw were very simple — and very inexpensive. The grandest room of the handful available was in a back corner of the building, with its own functional bathroom and some country antiques.

The wooden structure of the basic building is typical of the town, and reminiscent of the "old west" in the United States. The open windows are shuttered, and while that may keep out the brilliant sunlight, the street noises roar and can be unsettling.

When John Morris arrived by boat from New Zealand, he had no thought of running an inn. The place simply developed, from friends who stopped by and sailors who had heard about his place. Decor and atmosphere come from his ability to collect interesting remnants from the sea and the small villages. Relics hang from the walls and the ceiling (as is the case with an old hull).

Aimed toward nautical folk, the inn has proved to be a haven for the crew from the cruise ships that deposit their passengers in Puerto Plata on regular runs out of Miami, and for sailing folk who come in to get their land legs, a shower, and a good meal.

There are seven tables in the dining area where food is American, with Dominican touches. The lounge areas, around the bar, are colorful, punctuated with plants and decorated with the relics I've already mentioned.

Except for the tawdry Pepsi Cola sign that announces Hotel Castilla at the street corner, this inn is a unique gem that will intrigue repeat Caribbean visitors who like their havens a little off-beat.

HOTEL CASTILLA, John F. Kennedy #34, Puerto Plata, Dominican Republic. Telephone: Puerto Plata 586-2559. The 16 rooms are very simple, most without private bath. Room 11 is the most elaborate, because it has a mahogany bed and a few country antiques, plus a private bathroom of sorts. Rooms had overhead fans for breeze maneuvering when I visited; there are plans for air-conditioners in some rooms. Plans for refurbishing will pretty the place up, but the basic structure of the building precludes any elaborate (and heavy) additions for the second floor of this wood building.

Getting there: Once you've cleared customs at the International Airport near Santo Domingo on the south coast, take a taxi to Herrera Airport for the Alas del Caribe flight to Puerto Plata, or rent a car for the four-hour drive to the north coast. If you fly to Puerto Plata's new airstrip (and there may be direct flights from the States by the time of your visit), you'll have to take a taxi, or arrange in advance for a rental car, for the half hour drive west to the town of Puerto Plata.

FRENCH WEST INDIES

Two *départements* of France, both equal to those of mainland France, are warmed by the Caribbean sun: Martinique, an almond-shaped island with an infamous volcano at its northern quarter, and butterfly-shaped Guadeloupe, which is actually two island "wings" joined by a bridge "body" plus its satellite islands of Marie Galante, Désirade, St. Barthélemy, the French part of St. Martin and the eight islands known as Les Saintes all just south of Trois Rivières, Guadeloupe.

The two biggest islands—Martinique and Guadeloupe—are probably the best known, but the entire group is French to the core. Language and customs are obviously French; the Creole customs that lead to colorful native costumes and lively dances and parades for festive occasions make these islands unique under the Caribbean sun. Fishing provides a way of life, a purpose for special festivals, and the main ingredient for the unusual Creole cooking that makes gourmets stop at small wooden shacks for a sumptuous meal.

Tropical forests and national parks preserve the Caribbean flora, and provide places for hiking and botanic study; beaches that rim the coasts have proved to be push-off points for sportsmen in search of wrecks and reefs and explorers who study the underwater life.

Arriving by air on Guadeloupe and Martinique is direct from New York on American Airlines and via San Juan, Puerto Rico, with an Eastern Airlines connection. From Miami, Air France and Eastern make connections. Nonstop flights on KLM and Eastern touch Sint Maarten (Dutch side), from New York; flights also come north from Guadeloupe. For St. Barthélemy, the easiest route is to fly to Sint Maarten and take a 15-minute Winair flight to St. Barths from there. Air Guadeloupe and charter planes fly several times daily between Guadeloupe and Terre de Haut (one of Les Saintes islands) and Marie Galante; Cruise ships visit Fort-de-France on Martinique, Pointe à Pitre on Guadeloupe, Philipsburg (on the Dutch side) and Marigot (on the French side) of Sint Maarten/St. Martin, and occasionally at Gustavia, the harbor of St. Barthélemy.

Star attractions vary from the volcano and the museum of Mt. Pelée at St. Pierre on Martinique to the nudist beaches off Guadeloupe at Terre de Haut. There are beaches at St. Martin, along with bistros and fishing villages, and St. Barthélemy, which most people call St. Barths (pronounced St. Barts), has a special charm, the result of Swedish history and the customs of the early settlers from Brittany. All the islands, with the exception of pancake-flat Marie Galante, are hilly, verdant, beach-fringed and unmistakably French, from the cuisine and the customs to the carefree topless sunbathers on most beaches. French is the language of the country, and you'll have a better holiday if your French is fluent.

Action options are endlessly French. For daytime, there are the usual scuba, snorkel,. and sailing opportunitits—with instruction given in French-accented English when it is given at all and climbing the volcanoes on Martinique or Guadeloupe. Golf is available at the course near the village of Trois Ilets on Martinique, not far from the resort area at Pointe de Bout, a 20-minute boat trip across the bay from Fort-de-France. There's also a course on Guadeloupe, near the village of Saint François and the Meridien Hotel. Guests at St. Martin's inns can drive to the Dutch side's Mullet Bay Hotel course. For tennis, head for the bigger hotels on any island; most of them have courts.

Shops with French fashions and perfumes fill the streets of Fort-de-France, capital of Martinique, and Pointe à Pitre, the main city of Guadeloupe (where the town of Basse-Terre is the capital), but some of the most colorful island fashions can be found in the shops at Gustavia on St. Barths, or at boutiques in Marigot, the main town of French St. Martin.

Casinos capture the nightlife at the Meridien Hotels on both Martinique and Guadeloupe (and at big hotels on the Dutch side of Sint Maarten), but the local discos—some at hotels and others on their own in the hotel orbits—are the preferred activity to follow the French gourmet meals.

Best beaches are at coves around the two big islands of Guadeloupe and Martinique, not in the capitals or main towns, but around the rim and on the offshore islands. Terre de Haut and Marie Galante have good beaches; St. Martin has several long sandy strands with one of the best at Le Galion, not far from the village of Grand Case. Topless bathing is common on all French beaches and special areas are set aside for nudist bathing and sunning.

For further information, contact the French West Indies Tourist Board at 610 Fifth Avenue, New York, New York 10022. Telephone: (212) 757-1125. The Office Departemental du Tourisme is in Pointe à Pitre, Guadeloupe, French West Indies, or at Bord de Mer, Fort-de-France, Martinique, French West Indies. (You'll need 25¢ per half-ounce airmail for the French islands.)

AUBERGE ANSE MITAN, on the beach near all the Pointe de Bout hotels, right across the bay from Fort de France.

The location is ideal, and it has been the site of an inn for many years. Guests have all the activity of Pointe du Bout within a short walk, first along the beach and then along a path which becomes a road. There's the marina with all its boats, plus the cluster of big hotels, including the Meridien (with casino), the Frantel, and the Bakoua, all offering variety for evenings out (especially the Bakoua where food is authentic French West Indian and delicious). There are boats for charter, tennis courts for play, and the golf course nearby—plus the peace and quiet of a small inn outside the door of your room. Count on good creole cooking at the inn's dining room.

The beach is adequate, but not one of the Caribbean's best. Perhaps that's the price you pay for being next to all the action. Although you can get along with English, you'll be much happier with some French at your command, especially if you want to converse with the people you may meet when you wander off the well-worn American tourists' routes.

AUBERGE ANSE MITAN, Anse Mitan, Trois Ilets, Martinique, French West Indies. Telephone: 76.31.12. Guests in the 20 air-conditioned rooms with private bath/shower, in the three-story main building will find accommodations simple, adequate, but not remarkable. There are two one-bedroom cottages along the beach for those who want to be completely self-sufficient. A few rooms have a sea view.

Getting there: Same as for Caraibe Auberge: A choice of expensive (60 francs) taxi, or many changes by taxi or bus to Fort de France, and ferry to Anse Mitan (20-minute ride), at less than a third of the price of the direct cab route. It's about half an hour from Lamentin Airport.

CARAIBE AUBERGE, on the beach at Anse Mitan, across the harbor from Fort de France, Martinique, F.W.I.

It was sweet, fresh tamarind juice that Mme. Guatel brought to me along with her sincere welcome, when I sat in the sun that first morning on the patio. I was at the water's edge, and on the edge, as well, of the activity that percolates around the marina at Pointe de Bout, a short walk from the inn. French is the language of manners, mores, and conversation at Mme. Guatel's home-turned-inn. Guests can lounge on the beach or enjoy the casual atmosphere that is reminiscent of small Riviera towns on mainland France. The bustle of the capital, Fort de France, is a short ride on the ferry across the harbor.

While a Martinique friend of mine, Danielle Dongar, and I were talking with Mme. Guatel about how she happened to open this place, her grandson waved a greeting as he scampered by on his way to the beach. The inn is still Mme. Guatel's home, as it can be yours. She opened it to visitors, she said, when her husband passed away and she found herself with time on her hands.

You'll find this another "Do whatever you want to" kind of place, but if you want help about places to visit, Mme. Guatel stands ready. (One choice is the museum at Trois Ilets where Napoleon's Josephine lived as a young girl before she went with her first husband, Beauharnais, to Paris and from there to a place in world history.)

The house is relatively new. Its austere white stucco and boxy lines are softened by the friendly presence of Mme. Guatel.

CARAIBE AUBERGE, Anse Mitan, Trois Ilets, Martinique, French West Indies. Telephone: Martinique 76.30.18. The two-story white stucco building has 12 air-conditioned rooms, some facing the sea, all with private bathroom. Furnishings are very simple, but the atmosphere is homey and comfortable if you are familiar with French ways, or want to learn them.

Getting there: Your choice is to take a taxi (or public bus) to Fort de France to wait for the frequent ferry service for the 20-minute ride across the bay to Anse Mitan beach, where you can walk to the inn. Or you can take a taxi from Lamentin Airport, at more than three times the cost of the other route, about 60 francs for the half-hour ride.

LEYRITZ PLANTATION, at Basse Pointe in the mountains north of Martinique.

When *Gourmet* magazine ran a story about Leyritz Plantation a few years ago, Mme. Yveline de Lucy de Fossarieu vowed never again to hire only one top chef. Soon after the piece appeared, people were flocking to the inn in unprecedented numbers, all of them expecting the same gourmet cuisine that they had read about in the magazine. The chef, meanwhile, had left for a higher paying job at another hotel, offered to him after the article appeared.

Don't worry about the food. It will be good (as it is at most places on Martinique, especially the small ones with atmosphere and access to the sea and fresh fish). Instead, you might give some thought to the day-trippers that make this their luncheon goal when they head out in rental cars (or on tours) from Fort de France. After the groups have gone, you can have the place to yourself. That's when it is the best.

The lawns undulate around the property, sliding into lush tropical foliage that would take over completely if things were not carefully tended. Horseback riding is one activity offered to guests. Many guests are content to sit by the pool, wander around the gardens, read, or go off to a nearby beach with a picnic lunch and plenty of leisure time.

This is no place for rushing. There's a tennis court—and arrangements can be made with the Hotel Latitude for use of their waterskiing, snorkeling, scuba, and sailing equipment if you want more activity than an isolated beach can provide.

The main house is the most charming part of the complex, and that's where the common rooms are. Around the grounds are the former slave quarters, now refurbished with magazine photos used for wall paper, as was the case in slave days. New "slave units" have been built in the old style.

LEYRITZ PLANTATION, Basse Pointe, Martinique, French West Indies. Telephone: 75.33.08. There are 25 rooms, all with private bath/shower even when the rooms are small. The 10 rooms in the main house are my preference, though they vary in size and outlook. The slave buildings are the 15 cottages, each with a refrigerator. Five of the rooms are air conditioned, if you insist, but the mountain breezes will make days and nights cool enough for most people.

Getting there: Brace yourself for a long and winding ride, almost 40 miles north of Lamentin Airport at a taxi fare that hovers around 120 francs. If you make the trip by daylight and aren't exhausted, it's worth breaking it with a lunch or teatime stop along the road, perhaps near the Mt. Pelée Museum.

MANOIR DE BEAUREGARD, at Chemin des Salines, three miles inland from the coast, at the south of the island near Ste. Anne.
When you get here, you may either want to settle in or rent a car for a day or two to drive around. The heart of the inn is an 18th century home, refurbished but still furnished with the antiques you'd expect to find at an elegant plantation home. The main stone building is on a rise, with a pool cupped in an arbor on one side, and an area for al fresco dining on another side.

This is a place to relax with your favorite books, to revel in peace and quiet. There's no action, but plenty available nearby if you want to go to the Club Med. In the village of Ste. Anne, not far away, there are a few shops and bistro-style restaurants.

Speaking some French is a help; self-sufficient types who enjoy challenges can survive without it. The atmosphere encourages a private holiday experience, with a minimum of socializing with other guests. If the guests are total strangers when you arrive, chances are they will remain so when you leave, unless you are exceptionally outgoing—and they want to be, too.

A nice excursion from here is to drive along the coast, through the fishing village of Vauclin when the fishermen are selling their morning's catch, and on up to the windward coast near Le François, to Les Brisants, where you can enjoy a fresh broiled langouste (local lobster), with French West Indies punch, on the porch. Most of the countryside is rural and residential; it does not focus on tourists.

MANOIR DE BEAUREGARD, Chemin des Salines, Ste. Anne, Martinique, French West Indies. Telephone: Martinique 76.73.40. Fifteen of the 25 air-conditioned rooms are in a new building that stretches out behind the 18th century house. All rooms have antique furniture, most have two double beds, four-posters, and other comfortable furnishings, plus—for those in the wing—a small terrace area. The rooms in the manor house are homier, each with its own style, and all with modern facilities.

Getting there: Since the inn is almost 30 miles from Lamentin Airport, the taxi fare will be a staggering 108 francs, but once there, you can walk into Ste. Anne, and the nearest beach is only three miles away. Fort de France will be a place to visit on the day you rent a car. It, too, is about 30 miles from the inn.

RELAIS DE LA GRAND SOUFRIERE, St. Claude, Basse-Terre, Guadeloupe, F.W.I.

The meal was a feast! We had driven here from our hotel near the busier hub of action, Pointe à Pitre, up the coast through fishing villages, and along a wiggly, up and down route leading north to the capital of Guadeloupe, to the town of Basse-Terre. The Relais is in the hills, inland from the seaside town.

Eight of us sat at a table in the dining room overlooking the garden and the three-hour lunch began—with full French flair. The meal was perfectly served, from the soup through the fish course, to meat and on to the flaky pastries that were served for dessert.

This is one of the island's two hotel schools. Students, whose instructors stand nearby observing and correcting, prepare and serve the meals. Reservations are essential for meals at the Relais.

Used by Guadeloupe's prefect, the highest government official, while his own home was being renovated, the Relais is in the residential suburb of Guadeloupe's capital of Basse-Terre in an area known as St. Claude. Built as a private home, the inn retains that atmosphere. Each bedroom has its own personality, with special furnishings. Many have a view of the garden. Each room is named for a great hotel in metropolitan France. White doors open from a high-ceilinged hall.

The Relais is a quiet, country spot. Don't expect to find any nightlife. If there is some, it will probably be a private party. The place is popular with well-to-do families from Guadeloupe who come here to celebrate special occasions.

The area made headlines in the summer of 1976, when the volcano (called Soufrière, as are most volcanoes throughout the Caribbean) belched smoke and ash and seemed to threaten worse. Volcanologists who had been watching and charting its course have now agreed that all is calm. On my first visit to the town of Basse-Terre, on the northeastern coast, everything was peaceful, as it is once again.

RELAIS DE LA GRAND SOUFRIÈRE, St. Claude, Basse-Terre, Guadeloupe, French West Indies. Telephone: 81.41.27. The 20 split-level rooms are air-conditioned and if rooms can have personality, these do. Each has a private bath and modern furnishings. There is nothing to do in the evening, but it is a pleasant, quiet retreat (no beach or pool) on a hillside above the capital of Basse-Terre, a short distance from the volcano Soufrière. The nearest beach, Rocroy, is about 10 miles away.

Getting there: Car or car-driver is necessary for the 40-plus mile trip from Raizet Airport and Pointe à Pitre. Allow a good hour and a half. This is a good place to stop for lunch and relaxation on a day's excursion.

AU GRAND CORSAIRE, in the village of Gosier on Grand-Terre, Guadeloupe, F.W.I.

Stretching the announced definition of inns, I'm including this place with its eight small cottages—some call them bunga-lows—because the restaurant and beachside location make it a small bistro/inn in the best French tradition.

New owners were expected at the time of my visit, so that the furnishings—always simple—were in some cases downright tattered. But still, the aura of sea and sun that pours over this place, and the cooking magic of Yvon Kerguen, make a few days here ideal for readers who know and like the French Riviera.

As with most places in the French West Indies, speaking fluent French certainly adds to the holiday experience.

The cabins scamper up the hillside, away from the small

restaurant and the beach. A rental car is a solution if you want to be mobile, but if you bring enough books, you can settle in right here. Almost in the shadow of the small Catholic church in downtown Gosier, the churchbells make sleeping late impossible. You'll probably be up with the sun.

The onetime fishing village of Gosier has spurted into resort headlines during the past few years, when more than 500 hotel rooms were added to the spit of land that juts into the sea from Auberge de la Vieille Tour, the "first" hotel on this area and still one of the best. Today the village is a curious mixture—not always pleasing—of simple West Indian shacks and modern concrete boxy structures, some of each filled with the latest French fashions for sunny weather wearing.

If you stay here, however, you'll be in your bathing suit most of the time, except when you put on some coverup to walk down the hill to the beach.

AU GRAND CORSAIRE, Gosier, Guadeloupe, French West Indies. Telephone: Guadeloupe 841203. The 10 rooms are in eight separate bunglows and, although there's nothing fancy about appurtenances, the place is acceptable and will be very comfortable if you like French-style tropical vacations. All rooms have a view of the sea and a private bathroom-with-shower. If you want air-conditioning, ask for one of the 4 rooms that offer it.

Getting there: Five miles from Pointe à Pitre, and a 15-minute ride from the airport, the inn is best reached by taxi and you can expect to pay the French franc equivilent of about $7. The public bus, recommended only for adventuresome travelers, runs between Pointe à Pitre and Gosier. A ride costs about 2Fr (50¢).

BOIS JOLI, Terre de Haut, Les Saintes, F.W.I.

Small planes sweep in from Guadeloupe in about 30 minutes. There's also boat service, across the choppy sea from Guadeloupe's town of Trois Rivières which is at least an hour's drive from Guadeloupe's airport or the city of Pointe à Pitre. I suspect that the challenge of getting here is one of the reasons that this small island is still a quiet French haven for those of us who would rather contemplate sea and sand than nightclubs and slot machines.

No matter how you get here, as soon as you meet Jacques Bouny you'll feel right at home. Fleeing the commerce and confusion of Bordeaux, he came to Terre de Haut in 1970. There were only two cars on this small French island then, and the airstrip had been cleared for only three years. Today there are several flights daily between Guadeloupe's Le Raizet Airport and the airstrip on Terre de Haut, and about twenty cars on the island.

I found walking or boating the best ways to explore—to watch the boats dock in town (also called Terre de Haut), to watch the fishermen mend their nets, and to scramble around impressive Fort Napoleon, perched on a hilltop. The Fort is undergoing a face-lift, mostly thanks to volunteers who are members of the French Club de Vieux Manoir.

The small white stucco inn looks like a lump of sugar on a hillside, about a ten-minute drive from the airstrip. A "tarte d'amour" will be part of your welcome. It's a sweet cake that is a tradition on Terre de Haut and, if you've somehow resisted the children who sell them from baskets at the airport, a tarte will still be waiting, probably warm from the oven, when you arrive at Bois Joli.

Lodgings are either in the main house (a few rooms, dining room, terrace, front desk, and a small handcraft shop) or in cottages that spill down the hill onto the beach. The sandy shore slides into the sea, and I do too when I arrive.

A boat leaves from the dock at the whim of guests, to take you to a completely isolated beach around the cove. Or you can walk up and over the hill, following a path that meanders behind the "sugar lump" house.

Although Bois Joli is one of the "home" hotels for V.I.B. Tours, otherwise known as Vacations-in-the-Buff, Mme. Bouny plainly says in animated French that vacationing in the buff is "pas pour tout le monde," and is certainly not for her dining room, the hotel's own beach, or for her young children who call this inn home.

It's a family-style place, run informally with sun and sea the main entertainment. Guests keep coming back. They are mainly French plus a handful of Americans.

As for cuisine, Mme. Bouny will oversee the perfect preparation of the fish you catch, or you can dine from a menu of local fish, lobster, and island vegetables, prepared in the piquant sauces you would expect to find in a French household.

Francophiles take note: speaking French will certainly add to your holiday. It is possible to survive without it, but as a courtesy to your hosts, even a struggle to recall a bit of high school French will be appreciated.

BOIS JOLI, Terre de Haut, Les Saintes, F.W.I. Telephone: 128. A 21-room inn on a hillside, overlooking its own beach and within walking distance of several others. French-speaking owners assist with fishing, scuba diving, exploring, and other activities. Cottages near the beach are modern, with private bath; rooms in the main house are modest but comfortable. Some share a bath. Rates are moderate, with good values in summer or as part of a V.I.B. Tour.

Getting there: The several links are relatively easy, but do travel light. Fly to Guadeloupe to board the small plane to Terre de Haut. Getting there by boat is best arranged from Guadeloupe and is recommended only for hardy travelers.

EDEN ROCK, on a rock at the shore of Baie de St. Jean.

For your sake, I hope nothing has changed since my most recent visit to the Eden Rock. The lavish and extensive plans that Helen de Haenen has for the inn on a rock between two white sand bays, are impressive, but the place is a pearl as it is. Helen's father built it. As is true of most Caribbean inns, not everyone will share my enthusiasm for a place where "hot" water was warmed by the sun long before solar heating became fashionable, and where the antiques in every room are sun-and-surf worn, and watermarks border the frames of some of the prints. (Note the prints not only for the scenes and costumes they portray, but also for the fact that they were done by Helen's grandfather in the late 1800s, on commission for the Czar of Russia.)

Most of the people who come here have done so for years.

Eden Rock has attracted a select few wise enough to see the advantages of sun, peace, and quiet, without unnecessary flourishes. The atmosphere is homelike and comfortable, in the customary French tradition which means leaving you alone to follow you own inclinations. (Helen's ambitious plans include adding all modern conveniences to brand new rooms that will replace the present cottages, and an elegant, club-like atmosphere, but her plans will be only dreams until the season of 1979 at the earliest.)

Remy de Haenen, Helen's father, was for many years the Mayor of St. Barths. He used to fly his small plane to St. Maarten, or wherever needed, to pick up guests for his inn. He landed on the grass strip, now paved, that begins at a point between two hills and slants to the sea. (Short Take-Off and Landing planes, known as STOLS, sweep in from Sint Maarten with ease, and private planes can flit in and out at pilot-and-passenger whim.)

The Eden Rock I know as this is written (and have known for years) has a main house whose red roof is a welcoming beacon on the horizon, plus three nearby cottages that saunter down the slope as near as possible to the sea. The lounge areas are carved into the other side of the rock. They are cozy enough for two, perhaps a congenial four. You'll dine on the terrace and, while your meal may not be the impromptu fresh fish that Helen grilled when we realized that all restaurants were closed the day I arrived, it will surely be good. Dinner is served by starlight and candlelight.

EDEN ROCK, St. Jean, St. Barthélemy, French West Indies. Telephone: via Guadeloupe, 97.60.01. The 7 rooms are in the main house, where room 1 has a big four-poster bed and a good view, or in the three separate buildings that lean against each other as they seem to slip down from the top of the rock. Room 4 makes up with atmosphere what it may lack in modern conveniences (although there is a flush toilet and sun-warmed water for the shower). Its private deck is perfect for sunbathing or for watching the sea that spreads out before you and sloshes at your feet. Only a little imagination will let you believe you're far out to sea.

Getting there: Winair flies into St. Barths several times daily, in 15 minutes or less from nearby Dutch St. Maarten. There are also flights from Guadeloupe (Air Guadeloupe). From the airport, the drive to the inn takes about five minutes in a taxi or a rental car that you can pick up at the airport. The port of Gustavia is popular with sailors.

AUTOUR DU ROCHER, on the water at Anse de Lorient, the next bay east beyond St. Jean and the small airstrip.

I suspect, although those responsible may not be enthusiastic about the comparison, that Autour du Rocher took its cue from Remy de Haenen's successful and special resort, Eden Rock, near St. Barths airport. Autour du Rocher is also on a rise at the side of the sea. Its rooms, public and private, are scattered over the hilltop, but the center here is a green bower with monkeys in the trees and the "real" tropics at your fingertips, a courtyard around which the other buildings cluster.

This is a place for the self-sufficient, fluent in French and familiar with French customs. You are very much atop a rock, on your own, with the lovely bays below and the rest of the island on St. Barths to explore.

The view you see of mushroom-shaped buildings on a hillside across the bay is a Michelin-financed development that has slowed down in the past couple of years, but is likely to get into full gear again as enthusiasm for St. Barths increases.

AUTOUR DU ROCHER, Lorient, St. Barthélemy, French West Indies. Telephone: via Guadeloupe, 87.60.73 (if you call from Guadeloupe, there is no toll charge). The 8 rooms vary in appointments and comforts, but if you expect to find things very simple, you won't be disappointed. Views are spectacular, and you are just a short walk from a lovely beach at Lorient shore. Some of the rooms are in the main house (sun-heated water); others are in two separate bungalows (with hot and cold water).

Getting there: By car (rental or taxi) from the airport it takes less than 15 minutes, heading east along the north coast. You can reach St. Barths, as noted, in a 15-minute flight on Winair from St. Maarten, or in about an hour heading north from Guadeloupe on Air Guadeloupe.

LES CASTELETS, high in the hills, almost straight up from the town of Gustavia.

Once you get over the shock of the driveway that cants to this inn, you can muster all your superlatives for the view, the cuisine, the appointments and the place in general. Castelets is a gem, ably-managed by Mme. Geneviève Jouany.

It can be a true sybarite's dream, if the sybarite does not need a beach and the sea at his doorstep to enjoy the Caribbean (and I do). The lofty location supports the lofty air around the place; Les Castelets is not for everyone, and is not for anyone who isn't prepared to be chic, attractive and up to date on the latest international conversation.

Luxury is the last word—and the first word here. The cluster of white, stucco buildings seem simple, and are from the outside. Inside, nothing has been spared with the decoration. You can't help but marvel at how all this flair for fashionable surroundings got to this rook's nest in remote St. Barths. Chalk it up to the good sense and imagination of the French, and a lot of money—some American funds included.

There is a pool, but it is petit and discrete. Meals are served to house guests (on reservation only, for outsiders); they are elegant, gourmet affairs, by candlelight after nightfall. If you like your personal pleasures at a luxury level, and can afford it, try this inn.

LES CASTELETS, Mount Lurin, St. Barthélemy, French West Indies. Telephone: 876173. The 9 rooms are in several buildings. There are two 2-bedroom duplex units with kitchen area plus living room, balcony, and the bedrooms with private bath; another unit has three air-conditioned bedrooms, with a kitchenette and living room with a terrace; and then there are two small bedrooms in the main house. All the rooms have a complimentary bar and a tape deck.

Getting there: After you have flown from Sint Maarten to St. Barths (15 minutes via Winair flight), you can get a taxi to drive you to Gustavia and up the hill to this perch. The entire distance is about a mile, but it seems like more because of the roads and the ever-changing view.

GRENADA

It's all here: the sun, the sand, the sea, and some of the Caribbean's most alluring countryside. The 133 square miles of Grenada offer Caribbean nature at its best, with hillsides covered with spice plantations that give the island its own special flavor. Grenada has been a port of call for ships since pirateering days in the 18th century when French and British rallied for control of protected St. George's Harbour. Sailors in the 20th century have anchored at St. George's, and at coves around the country's south coast, often using the ports as landfall after a cruise with the prevailing trade winds down the chain of Grenadine Islands from St. Vincent, the island at the north.

When independence was granted by England in 1974, the country grappled with its identity. The decision was made to revitalize efforts for tourism, encouraging visitors to get to know the country and the Grenadians through the many small hotels and inns. English traditions are gradually becoming Grenadian. The local language is distinctly English, albeit with a Grenadian lilt. Life thrives at the weekly market, held in St. George's against a backdrop of sun-bleached wooden houses with pastel roofs and the curve of the town wharf as it meets the sea.

Arrival is by boat (usually a cruise ship) or by plane. From Barbados, connections can be made for the service that makes the one-hour flight to Grenada. To reach Carriacou and Petit Martinique, two of the Grenadine Islands that are governed from Grenada, there is mail boat service. A small plane also flies from Grenada's Pearls Airport to Carriacou.

Star attractions are the spectacular powdery sand beaches on the south coast, the lush countryside in the interior and a Caribbean town with its traditional architecture intact as its capital.

Activities are sea-oriented, with sailing leading the list. There's not a lot of planned activity. Tours by taxi take you to fishing villages, verdant hillsides, a visit to a spice factory, a glimpse at Grand Etang, a crater lake, and the prospect of a swim at one of the sandy coves. Tennis is a favorite sport of the Premier, Eric Gairy. Courts are available at many of the hotels. There's no golf course.

Nightlife is limited to the hotels, where you may find a steel band or another island singing group. Dinner hour will be the main activity, and pub life, complete with darts, is the way to spend a casual evening.

Best beaches are on the south coast, and the expanse at Grand Anse (Big Beach) is the best known. There are good beaches at most south coast coves, and all beaches everywhere are open to the public.

For further information, contact the Caribbean Tourist Association, 20 East 46th Street, New York, New York 10017. Telephone: (212) 682-0435. In Grenada, the Tourist Board is located at Box 293, St. George's, Grenada, West Indies. (25¢ postage per half-ounce airmail.)

CALABASH, on the beach at L'Anse aux Epines, about five miles south of the town of St. George's.

As with many Caribbean inns, it is the group that gathers around the open-air wining and dining area, with its "roof" of tropical growth, that makes this place special. The directors' chairs that you pull up to your dining table may be sun-bleached and wobbly, but the comraderie that you feel from the other guests when the house is full is substantial.

Calabash was opened in 1964, by Englishman Brian Thomas who ran it for several years. It was a favorite gathering place for the yachting types that used to flock to Grenada in the halcyon days before independence. Today, the visitors that come to Grenada are often here on business and they mingle with residents and the handful of tourists here and at other Grenadian inns.

The name for the inn comes from a gourd-like fruit that grows on trees here and throughout the Caribbean. In the old days the calabash was cut in half to be used as a bowl or container; these days, the Calabash Inn contains hospitality, in a relaxed atmosphere. Excellent island food is served at mealtimes.

Charles de Gale, the Grenadian who now owns and operates the inn, will share his knowledge of what has been known for centuries as the "Spice Island," and will see that each member of the staff provides the information and the service that will enable you to enjoy your vacation. In spite of the fact that the rooms are in several cottages around the grounds on Prickly Bay, the feeling here is that of a small, well-run inn.

CALABASH HOTEL, Box 382, St. George's Grenada, West Indies. Telephone: Grenada 4234. The 22 suites are in ten cottages scattered around eight acres, beachside about five miles south of St. George's. Each of the units has a twin-bedded room, bathroom and sitting room area, as well as a kitchenette and porch. Louvered windows open your room to the breezes. One unit has its own pool. Construction is a tropical combination of stucco and wood, with comfortable, but not lavish, furnishings. A few of the suites are upstairs in a two-story unit; but most are on ground level, an easy walk to the beach.

Getting there: Fly to Barbados to connect with a plane for Grenada (either charter a small plane for the 45-minute flight, or take the scheduled service, if its schedule happens to fit yours). From the airport, count on about an hour taxi drive to the hotel. (Incidentally, L'Anse aux Epines is pronounced, vaguely, as "Lance-eh-pan").

HORSESHOE BAY HOTEL, spilling downhill to its own beach, a few miles out of St. George's and about an hour's drive from the airport.

My first visit here was not long after John and Agnes Yearwood opened their luxury hotel a few years ago, and before it was sold to the Hopkins brothers in late 1977. The architecture suggests Spanish Colonial style with white stucco and tile roofs, but everything else is pure West Indian. The main building, the first you step into, is at the top of the hill, with living units off to the right as you face the sea. The terrace and dining room open out to the view, with the fresh-water pool farther down, and the beach rimming the shore.

Although there is planned entertainment some evenings in the winter season, Horseshoe Bay appeals primarily to those in search of peace and quiet (including honeymooners). A steel band is featured some evenings; otherwise it's darts, snooker, cards, backgammon, and getting to know the other guests.

Grenada's verdant countryside offers some unusual touring if you want to take a cab for a day, but you will already have seen most of the terrain on your trip from the airport. The town of St. George's is worth a wander, not only for its several small shops (some with fine handcrafts) but also for its lively waterfront life. Island schooners selling goods are fun to watch. The island market is open every day, but is at full tilt on Saturday morning.

For sports in the sun at the Horseshoe Bay beach, you can take out a Sunfish or a Windsurfer, plus a rowboat—all free. Snorkeling is a special delight right off the shore, and arrangements can be made for scuba, and deep-sea fishing, and one-day-or-longer, big boat sailing to some of the nearby Grenadines.

HORSESHOE BAY HOTEL, Box 174, Lance Aux Epines, Grenada, West Indies. Telephone: Grenada 4410. The rooms are elegant, furnished with antique-style four-poster beds. Each room has its own efficiency unit and laundry area, used by the hotel staff to cook your breakfast and do your laundry. (You may use it too, if you choose.) The 12 spacious rooms are in six units and are more like villas than "cottages."

Getting there: Once you've arrived in Grenada, you'll have the same hour-long ride through the countryside that you have for all the small inns. "Everything" for visitors is located on the south shore, not too far from the town of St. George's.

SPICE ISLAND INN, tucked into an estate that borders the Caribbean at Grand Anse Beach.

The Grenadian/Canadian Company that owns and operates this unique spot has a prize property on its hands. The 1200 feet of beachfront are almost enough to make the inn perfect, but the tropical atmosphere that pervades the main house, the beach building, the 20 ocean front beach suites and the 10 pool

suites lure repeaters who have continued to come to Grenada through the vagaries of independence, "growing pains" and the fluctuating schedules of the small planes that fly between Barbados and this southern speck.

Although the cottages at Spice Island are basic board-and-glass construction, there's elegance offered with your own private swimming pool, and the carefully-tended flowers and plants that flourish around the grounds.

One of the top attractions with this spot is the beach, a long stretch of powdery sand that is wide enough to provide places for all who want to swim here. The units are set back in the tropical growth that fringes the strand so that Spice Island's guests can enjoy their privacy.

SPICE ISLAND INN, Box 6, St. George's, Grenada, West Indies Telephone: Grenada 4258 or 4244. My room preference is one of the 20 beachfront suites, each tucked into the tropical growth, although the 10 pool suites, each with its own small pool, are preferred by some repeaters. Rooms are comfortably furnished with simple, outdoor-style furniture. There's nothing lavish, but the inn is beach-comfortable.

Getting there: Fly to Grenada from Barbados (about a 45-minute flight), and then take a taxi to Grand Anse Beach and the Spice Island Inn. When you are here, you will be about a 20-minute drive from St. George's.

SECRET HARBOUR, capping the slope that rises from Mt. Hartman Bay.

Even before the official opening in 1971, I overnighted in one of the very special rooms here at Secret Harbour, reveling in the glorious view that surrounded me as I stood on my balcony. The living portion of my room had the couch conveniently placed so that I could sit and gaze at the Caribbean; behind is the bedroom, with its two double beds, both mahogany four-posters.

Secret Harbour is just that — a secret harbour for those who want a peaceful, quiet holiday in carefully pruned surroundings. Its main building, built in what is referred to in the islands as "Mediterranean style," has plenty of white-washed stucco walls, wrought iron accents, heavy wood beams, and carefully placed tiles. The feeling is one of open-air elegance, but the atmosphere is casual and comfortable.

You can lounge around the swimming pool, looking over your toes at the spectacular Caribbean that stretches out several feet below you. If you want more action, there's a pitch-and-putt golf course and some tennis courts for play.

Owner/manager Barbara Stevens gets most of the credit for keeping the caliber high at this inn which she built from the ground up. She has the help of Godfrey Ventour whose own contributions for the care and feeding of guests are considerable.

The curve of beach which you can look down on from poolside is a "long" walk down and around, especially if you've collapsed into the languuorous life that overwhelms many when they hit the Caribbean climate. That's your only chance to dunk in the Caribbean, however, unless you rent a car or hire a taxi to go to the marvelous strand known as Grand Anse Beach, or to the nearer, smaller but still glorious bays of L'Anse aux Epines over the hill toward town.

SECRET HARBOUR, Box 11, St. George's, Grenada, West Indies. Telephone: Grenada 4439 or 4548. The 20 suites at this special spot are all similar. All have a spectacular view, 2 double four-poster beds (some of them antique and others excellent copies), a beautifully tiled bathroom with all modern conveniences, and a sitting area that is comfortably furnished and will quickly become a home away from home. There are two suites in each of the 10 separate units that curve around the sea-side of the hilltop, so views are breathtaking.

Getting there: Fly to Grenada from Barbados or St. Lucia, and take a taxi for the hour long drive from Pearls Airport toward the capital of St. George's. Mt. Hartman Bay is about a 20-minute drive from town.

ROSS POINT INN, about two miles outside St. George's, following the coast along the southwest peninsula.

When Audrey and Curtis Hopkin opened their small inn in 1952, they gave many of us with no roots in Grenada a place to "come home" to. Capping its hill, with a view of the sea and the surrounding countryside, Ross Point is a home-turned-inn. With eldest son Royston Hopkin who has been active in the Caribbean Hotel Association and in other area promotions assisting with management, the inn promises to stay that way.

Although visitors can pick their own diversions during the daytime (swimming, sailing, tennis, walking, or visiting townships), most convene here in the evenings, along with the Grenadians who recognize the good food served. You can be assured of one of the best, and most authentic, West Indian meals you'll ever eat when you pull your chair to a table in the Ross Point dining room.

When you're ready for more than the view of St. George's, one of the Caribbean's most photogenic harbors, you can go into town, or ride the daily transport offered from the inn to the Hopkin's Beach Cottage on the sandy strand known as Grand Anse Beach.

ROSS POINT INN, Box 137, St. George's, Grenada, West Indies. Telephone: Grenada 4551. There are 12 rooms, each with its own personality. All rooms help preserve the homey quality of the inn. Rooms have air-conditioning (although it isn't really needed), private baths, and balconies overlooking a vast expanse of the Caribbean.

Getting there: As with most Grenada hotels, you will have had an island tour on your drive from the airport to Ross Point. The ride takes about an hour, and goes through some of the island's most verdant scenery. Count on a taxi fare of about $12 U.S. The easiest way to fly to Grenada is via Barbados with change there to the small LIAT plane that makes several daily flights (a 45-minute flight).

MERMAID INN, in the village of Hillsborough, on Carriacou.

Although this island is the largest of the Grenadines, it's actually a tiny dot of land known mostly to sailors — and not to too many of them. The inn was the home of J. Linton Rigg for many years. A yachtsman and writer, he moored himself on Carriacou in the 1960s, his twilight years. The inn was later taken over by Tom Vickery from Long Island, New York, and now is under the direction of Trevor and Hazel Ann Kent, who continue their predecessors' custom of running it in a comfortably casual way.

Make no mistake about it, this is an island outpost with only the two-street-wide village of Hillsborough and miles of beach and acres of ocean to keep you occupied. The inn is simple and is run, the Kents say, as an "old-style, West Indian hotel, with good food and an atmosphere of friendly intimacy, both typical of our island."

The island itself is bigger than you might expect at first. It is worthwhile taking a taxi-tour to see what's where. You'll find long stretches of beach, small hillside villages, farming plots, and a seemingly self-sufficient, small-island life. (Be sure to go up to the Princess Royal Hospital, either by taxi or on your own. The view over the cannon is one you won't soon forget!)

Day sailing or longer cruising is easily arranged, usually with some of the local folk or with those from afar who have chosen to drop anchor at nearby Tyrell Bay.

MERMAID INN, Hillsborough, Carriacou, Grenada, West Indies. Cable: KENT MERMAID, CARRIACOU, GRENADA, WEST INDIES (there is no telephone). There are 10 rooms at modest rates, including breakfast and dinner. If you insist on a private bath, you will pay a premium and you must specify this preference when you make your reservation. Most rooms have a shared bath.

Getting there: Now you'll see why this place is an outpost! Unless you sail in (which is certainly the easiest means of getting there), your choices include a flight to Barbados, with change to a small plane for the flight to Grenada. Then, and make sure it's still operating, you switch to Inter-Island Air Services Ltd. for the five-minute flight to Carriacou, or you can take the mail boat from Grenada to Carriacou (scenic but slow). Or you can fly south from St. Vincent, also on IIAS. Or, finally, charter a flight from Barbados direct to Carriacou. If you are in a group, the latter is certainly worth the cost.

HAITI

HAITI

The Caribbean's first black republic has been an independent country since it threw off the yoke of the French in 1804. For the independent traveler in search of the exotic, this country has the atmosphere that adds experience to the myths. If poverty bothers you, stay away from downtown Port au Prince; if the unusual intrigues you, search in the corners of the country.

The 60 mile by 100 mile mass of Haiti occupies one-third of the island of Hispaniola; the Dominican Republic claims the other two-thirds. Haiti's crab claw peninsulas at the north and south reach west toward Cuba.

Carrying their poverty with dignity, the Haitians are some of the Caribbean's most beautiful people. There's music in their souls, a smile on their faces, and art in their hearts as they continue a vibrant local culture of painting, dancing, wood-carving, and mystical mountain village voodoo.

Although the interior is seldom visited by outsiders, visitors are now finding their way out of the cauldron of humanity that is the capital of Port au Prince, to enjoy the Victorian gingerbread architecture of the south coast village at Jacmel as well as the northern Citadelle, built by more than 200,000 slaves at the command of the country's first native-born ruler, Henri Christophe.

Arriving on Haiti is easy via American Airlines out of New York and Miami, as well as on Eastern Airlines via Puerto Rico. Local flights stretch from the Port au Prince International Airport to Cap Haitien and to Jacmel. Cruise ships out of Miami and other United States ports visit Cap Haitien and the capital, Port au Prince.

Star attractions are the Citadelle (well worth enduring the jolting ride on the back of a donkey for the hour's climb to reach it), the countryside, and the Haitians themselves. The Haitian elite have a culture all their own, with the polish of continental France and the vibrance of their African-Caribbean heritage. Expect the unexpected. Haiti is not the traditional "paradise island." Abject poverty rubs shoulders with incredible wealth; overcrowded downtown Port au Prince is surrounded by wide open, rolling countryside with pockets of people where you least expect them. Recently improved roads thread along the coast for the hour-long-or-longer ride to the sandy coves nearest to the capital. Jacmel is a 4-hour ride on a well-paved road; the route to the north coast Citadelle from the capital is still a long poke, although the new road brings that ride from its former eight hours to a more reasonable three.

Action options include touring, lounging around the pools at the character inns, a game of tennis at one of the hotel-owned tennis courts (small fee for non-guests), or hours spent searching for colorful, primitive paintings, and handcarved wood figures and furniture.

Nighttime action will focus on the casino, a voodoo show at one of the hotels or at Le Peristyle, or a quiet dinner in one of Haiti's elegant, small restaurants.

Beaches should not be your reason for coming to Haiti. There are bands of sand bordering the west coast, north of Port au Prince, and the south coast near Jacmel as well as at the north coast, a short drive from Cap Haitien, but no beach I've seen in Haiti compares with some of those in, for example, the British Virgin Islands or the Grenadines.

For further information, the Haiti Government Tourist Office is at 30 Rockefeller Plaza, New York, New York 10020. Telephone: (212) 757-3517. In Haiti, the Office Nacional du Tourisme et de la Propagande is in Port au Prince, Haiti, West Indies. (25¢ postage per half-ounce airmail.)

HOTEL CRAFT, on the south shore at the town of Jacmel, about two hour's drive from Port au Prince and the airport.

After Marlene had overseen the lunch we were served on a recent visit to the craft, Erick Danies showed us through the hotel, discussing his plans for improvements and changes. I hope he hasn't accomplished any of them, not because I don't wish him well, but because his childhood home, where his family has lived for years, is charming just the way it is. I'm not sure that efficiency units and a private bath in each room would really improve it.

If you are lucky enough to see the Hotel Craft as I saw it (it began life as the Pension Craft), you should know that what is now the dining room was once the office of Erick Danies' grandfather, a European with a business in Haiti. Wide wooden stairs lead up from the front hall. The pictures that are on the walls as you climb the steps are of family members. The interesting, carved woodwork was done by a farmer who lives in the mountains nearby. He was a fine craftsman, and his style is Haitian primitive, the style reminiscent of many paintings you will see in Haiti.

People who come to Jacmel for the day lounge on the porch or in the airy dining room, where you'll find reed-and-wood Haitian chairs and delicious Haitian food.

If you are lucky enough to stay overnight, dinner will be by candlelight. The town of Jacmel provides most of the entertainment, with its market, a few art galleries (most notably Selman Rodman's home which is also his gallery) and a stretch of shoreline that is referred to as a beach but hardly compares to most other Caribbean beaches. The best stretches of sandy shore are a few miles away. Erick Danies knows where they are and he'll tell you how to find them.

HOTEL CRAFT, Jacmel, Haiti, W.I. Telephone: not available. The hotel had 12 rooms of varying sizes, shapes, and facilities when I was there, but they may be modernized by the time you arrive. Rooms 8 and 9 face the sea overlooking the town square, with an upstairs wrought iron balcony that is typical of many Haitian homes.

Getting there: It's a long trip even with the new roads, but you'll think it's easy when you realize that the journey used to take most of a day (at least eight hours on a rutted and often dissolving road). Now the winding route is a two-hour drive. Take a taxi for your first trip. Perhaps you'll want a rental car after that, but Haitian formalities make taxis easier and the fare is not bad.

MANOIR ALEXANDRE, stretching up a slope between the shore-level road and the road that fringes the village park at Jacmel.

A private home turned inn, Manoir Alexandre is still run like a residence where you are welcome to spend the night and to take your meals at the family table. You should speak French to do so comfortably (no one expects you to know the local patois). The house once belonged to a wealthy German who left the island in 1910. Since that time, a French family took over and they are still the owners.

The facilities are simple but pleasing. There's a porch for basking in the tropical breezes and watching the sun on the waters off the south coast of Haiti.

The area around Jacmel is off the usual tourist path. Daytime diversions can include exploring the south coast, finding some of the beaches outside of town, visiting the art galleries in the village (Naders is a branch of a Port au Prince gallery, and Selman Rodman's collection is shown in his house on the lower road), and going to the market, which takes place at the town square most mornings.

MANOIR ALEXANDRE, Jacmel, Haiti, W.I. Telephone: not available. There are 8 rooms of all sizes and shapes. A few have private bath, but most are simple bedrooms in a private home, with minimal extras but all the necessities.

Getting there: It's a long trip after a flight to Haiti's airport near Port au Prince, so you might consider including a few days in the city or at Pètionville to rest up so you can enjoy the two-hour drive. The French-built road, completed in 1977, is well-paved although winding, and the scenery is spectacular. Arrange for the taxi to pick you up if you are sure of your departure day and time. It may be hard to find a taxi in Jacmel.

HOSTELLERIE DU ROI CHRISTOPHE, perched on a hilltop at Cap Haitien, the fabled northern town of Haiti.

For those who follow Caribbean legends, this place will be a special treat. Not only was this a home for Napoleon's sister, Pauline Le Clerc and her General-husband whom Napoleon sent here to rule, but it was also Henri Christophe's jail, after he had defeated the French in 1811 and proclaimed himself King Henry I. The house had been built in 1724 as home for French Governor de Chatency, and it still looks the part.

The architecture is not the wood fretwork style called "gingerbread" that you may have heard about for Port au Prince hostelries, but it is a sturdy stucco bulwark with a grand entrance. As a hotel, it was completely spruced up a few years ago so that its bedrooms are comfortable and the appurtenances relatively modern.

I won't go so far as to call it "the jewel of Cap Haitien" which its management claims it to be, but I can say that if you make your way to this northern town with all its history, you should certainly stop in here. The management claims that many of the guests are private pilots who have winged into the runway at Cap Haitien. So if that sounds like your crowd, this is a place to try.

There is a pool on the grounds, but leisure time is often spent reading in a chair on the breezy, tiled verandah.

HOSTELLERIE DU ROI CHRISTOPHE, Cap Haitien, Haiti, West Indies. Telephone: not available. There are 18 rooms which vary in decor according to their location around the mansion. Furnishings are sparse, but beds are usually comfortable and each room has a private bathroom.

Getting there: The new road cuts the driving time from Port au Prince to about four hours, but that is still a long haul, after you've cleared customs at the Port au Prince Airport. It is possible to fly by small plane to the airport at Cap Haitien, and then take a taxi to the hotel. Flights connect Port au Prince and Cap Haitien.

MONT JOLI, about 5 minutes from the center of town at Cap Haitien, Haiti's northern town that is a 4-hour ride or a half hour flight from Port au Prince.

The place has grown like Topsy since its first modest beginnings, and today Mont Joli has the makings of a marvelous inn—with exceptional hospitality included in the reasonable rates.

The hub of the inn was a private home when it first stood tall on the hillside on the outskirts of town. Modern additions have put air-conditioning into the bedrooms, and added some new rooms as appendages, but it was impossible—thank heavens— to destroy the unusual Haitian architecture that gives this place its heart and soul.

Owners Walter and Mary Bussenius (she's Parisian) have been active in the Caribbean Hotel Association and know how to maintain a good island inn. Casual comfort is the key, and what this place lacks in beachside location it more than makes up for with good Haitian-style food and a spectacular view. There is transportation daily, departing at 9 a.m. and returning by 3 p.m., to a nearby beach if you insist. Men won't need a jacket and tie, but guests are expected to dress in "proper" attire for this casual spot. There's a tennis court, but don't count on finding tournament play or conditions.

The spectacular "extra" for Mont Joli, in addition to the owners, is the option to visit Haiti's magnificent Citadelle, created by Henri Christophe over the dead bodies of thousands of Haitians. It is proudly noted as the "Eighth Wonder of the World" in all printed literature about the country (most of it written or promoted by the Haitians themselves).

MONT JOLI, Cap Haitien, Haiti. Cable: HOTEL MONT JOLI CAP HAITIEN HAITI W.I. (There is no phone). The 22 rooms in the main part of the inn have private bath; many have terrace or balcony as well. Some rooms are called deluxe, but I've found the regular rooms more than adequate. For those who want more independence than this outpost grants in its inn, there are

6 villas, each with 3 bedrooms and full kitchen, living room, dining room and 2½ baths.

Getting there: By far the most pleasant route, if you can work it, is a one-way passage on the Norwegian Caribbean's Cruise that stops here, picking up the return to Miami on another cruise. If you can't work that (and at high season you probably can't), you'll have to put up with either the long (4 hours, but it seems longer) ride from Port au Prince, or the off-again-on-again airline service that runs on a schedule best known to itself. You should be flexible with your travel times; the airline is.

MARABOU HOTEL, on a side street in the town of Pétionville, up the hill from Port au Prince.

Mme. Odette Weiner is the reason that everything here runs so smoothly. She is Haitian, a dedicated dancer as well as an elegant hostess. She remains in the background except when she knows the guests. Her hotel is small and individual. It's not for the person who needs a lot of personal attention. Adventuresome travelers who want an inn in a small village in the hills of Haiti will be happy here.

The facilities are comfortable. An open lobby has several places to curl up with a book. There's another area in the back, near the dining room, that's more like a den.

The dining room is stark; the food pure Haitian and served only to guests who let the management know in the morning if they plan to be around later in the day for meals other than breakfast.

The pool at the side of the hotel is used only by guests. It is not large, but big enough for a dunk after a hot day of downtown touring in the city of Port au Prince.

MARABOU HOTEL, Pétionville, Haiti, W.I. Telephone: 71934. The 16 rooms are clean, but simple. Some are twin-bedded; others smaller and single. Ask for a room that opens onto the pool if you like the convenience of a quick dip.

Getting there: The taxi from the airport to Pétionville hotels will cost you about $6; allow almost 45 minutes for the ride from the airport on the fringe of Port au Prince up to the hill-side suburb.

OLOFFSON HOTEL, on a street with other Victorian houses in Port au Prince.

The fact that Oloffson's was one of the settings used in Graham Greene's novel *The Comedians* (a controversial book in Haiti) hardly caused a head to turn here at the inn. Oloffson's expects to be written about; many of the guests are writers and other professionals who like the extraordinary atmosphere.

Al Seitz is an expatriate from Connecticut. He and Suzanne make this place run like a top, but without much in the way of obvious flourishes. A boutique that has been added in recent seasons (called Bagaille, meaning "everything" in Creole) is a branch of another shop Suzanne Seitz runs with a colleague. The other one is up the hill on the way to Pétionville.

A pool was added a few years ago, to the right of the entrance as you go up the steps. Other than that, very little has changed. People like this place exactly the way it is.

When you walk up the front steps, you enter the lobby (there should be a better word, but nothing seems quite right for this special place). The chairs that slouch around the tables are wicker or wood, covered with calico. Tropical foliage oozes into the lobby and through the public rooms, even into the dining area where it punctuates the walls. Decor in the main area is nooks, books, and backgammon, with Haitian paintings and music to add a lively tone. You can read a book or do what you will — no one will care, as long as you're quiet about it.

OLOFFSON HOTEL, Port au Prince, Haiti, W.I. Telephone: 20139. The 24 rooms offer lots of variety but not much in the way of luxury. If you want fast-paced action, you'll be happier elsewhere. But if you want a place with much more personality than most (overhead fans in most rooms and air conditioning only when there's no circulation at all) and very rustic surroundings, this is it. Room 11 is the best; it's a classic—a suite with a balcony that is in one of the corner "turrets" of the inn, overlooking pool and gardens.

Getting there: Take a taxi from the airport and expect to pay about $5 for your ride. After the stretch from the airport to the edge of town, you will wiggle around and through a lot of small back streets. Don't worry. That's the only way the get there.

JAMAICA

The 144 by 49 miles of this country offer some of the Caribbean's most spectacular landscape and coastline. Independent since August 1962, the country's natural friendship with Cuba—some 200 miles off Jamaica's north shore—has led to cultural, economic, and ideological exchanges that have made North American headlines. Premier Michael Manley, reinstated as Premier in a landslide vote in 1977, leads his country along a path of democratic socialism that includes an egalitarian tourism program in which Jamaicans share with the outside world the resorts and holiday facilities of the country.

One of the first winter retreats for beleaguered northerners at the turn of the century when the banana shipping port of Port Antonio on the country's northeast coast was the hub of holiday activity, Jamaica has played host to visitors from other countries for all of its history. First there were the plantation owners who spent part of the year in their Caribbean outpost, but left the land to overseers the rest of the time. Tourism of the 1970s is different from those days. Most of the inns and hotels rim the north coast, around the town hubs of Ocho Rios, Montego Bay, and, once again, Port Antonio. A new area, which came into focus for Jamaican government tourism planning, is Negril, with a stretch of sandy coast at the northwest.

Arriving is easy by air and cruise ship. Direct and often nonstop flights on Air Jamaica touch Montego Bay and Kingston from U.S. east coast and midwestern cities. Connections make flights easy from the west coast. American Airlines also flies to Jamaica. Trans Jamaican Airlines is the local carrier that connects the island airports at Ocho Rios, Port Antonio, and Negril with the international airports at Kingston and Montego Bay. Cruise ships, many of them from Miami and some from New York, include Kingston, Montego Bay, Ocho Rios, and Port Antonio on itineraries.

Star attractions in Jamaica are beaches and the resort life, but a far more interesting holiday awaits those who spend some time in the country talking to the new Jamaicans, the young people who have grown up with independence. Kingston is not a tourist spot; it is a seething, bubbling Caribbean city with all the advantages (and disadvantages) of cities in any country. Montego Bay and Ocho Rios have plenty of the shops that are the traditional lure for Caribbean visitors, but most visitors will find the quieter, more natural pleasures of rafting on the Rio Grande or fishing out of Negril more to their liking. All are easily arranged, as are beach parties, by a branch of the Jamaica Tourist Board charged with the responsibility of "attractions."

Action options are endless. You can climb Dunn's River Falls as one of a human chain or on your own with a guide; you can raft on the Rio Grande near Port Antonio; you can go to a Jamaican barbecue by dugout canoe on the White River; or you can go deep sea fishing, take a scuba course, sail, play tennis, or play golf at one of the country's several excellent courses (Tryall course west of Montego Bay, Rose Hall course east of Montego Bay, the Upton Country Club near Ocho Rios, and several others). Horseback riding is offered at resort towns on the north coast.

Best beaches are along the north coast, with the miles (some say it's seven miles) of beach that run north of the village at Negril the best of the lot. There are isolated and relatively unknown coves on the south shore; most of the north coast beaches are freckled with hotels, but all beaches are open to the public.

For further information, the Jamaica Tourist Board's main U.S. office is at 866 Second Avenue, New York, New York 10017. Telephone: (212) 688-7660. In Jamaica, there are Tourist Board offices at all the resort towns. You'll find them at Cornwall Beach in Montego Bay, in Ocho Rios, and in Port Antonio. The head office of the Jamaica Tourist Board is at 80 Harbour Street, Kingston, Jamaica, West Indies. (25¢ postage per half-ounce airmail.)

BONNIE VIEW, about 600 feet up into the mountains, overlooking the harbor at Port Antonio.

Peace and quiet reigns supreme at this mountainside perch. The first turn out of town takes you up a steep and narrow village road, past small houses teeming with small children, but within a few minutes, you are up and overlooking all the sea-oriented action below. The stillness is almost overwhelming if you arrive at mid-day "quiet time" as I did on a recent visit.

The building you see first looks like the home it once was, with a terrace that looks over the village 600 feet below, and

benches around the grounds for pensive times. The tennis court that is near the parking area did not look as though it had seen much action, but it is there—such as it is—if you feel like playing.

There's a swimming pool at the back of the inn, beyond the rooms and in a gardened area with a view of the Blue Mountains beyond. The public rooms, at the front of the building up the stairs from the parking area, are open-air, West Indian simple. The place is clean, neat, and typically country-Jamaican, with good local food served at mealtimes.

It's a 15- or 20-minute drive down the hill to the nearest beaches, or to visit the spectacular Blue Lagoon, or to step aboard one of the rafts for a ride on the Rio Grande, a popular daytime sport. But you can also sit at this high-level spot to enjoy the peace and quiet with a book in hand and not go down hill at all until you leave to go home.

Bonnie View is understandably popular with Jamaicans who come here for lunch, dinner, the afternoon, or for weekends, and holidays at Port Antonio. For good value, the place offers one of the best bargains in Jamaican hotels.

BONNIE VIEW, Port Antonio, Jamaica, W.I. Telephone: Port Antonio 752. There are 30 rooms, most of them in a motel-style wing that stretches off the "back" of the inn, away from the view. A few rooms are over the public rooms in the main house, and there's a 2-bedroom cottage with a kitchenette which is economical for a family. Count on things being neat, clean, and very simple.

Getting there: If you rent a car at Montego or Kingston, you can drive here in about 3 hours from Kingston, and close to five or six hours along the north coast east from Montego Bay. Other possibilities are to fly Trans-Jamaican, the domestic airline, to Port Antonio from your probable arrival airport of Kingston or Montego Bay, and then find a taxi to take you for the 15-minute drive through Port Antonio and up the hill to Bonnie View. If you come in on a cruise ship, make reservations in advance for lunch here and taxi up from the ship's docking area.

DE MONTEVIN LODGE, at the corner of Musgrave Street, up the hill in the heart of Port Antonio.

If you like old West Indian houses that have maintained the traditions of the past, this inn is the place to see. Mr. Mullings, the owner of De Montevin, told me that he calls his place a "private hotel" because he discourages afternoon visits. This is a place, he told me, for a husband and wife or for family types.

The Mullings, a Port Antonio family, took the place over in 1959, and have carefully maintained the Victorian house with all its flourishes. The coats of paint that keep the place looking clean and neat have not covered up the details carved into the fretwork, or the special trimmings around the doors, arches, and louvered windows.

There's a front porch for rocking, and an over-stuffed parlor room that looks as it probably looked a couple of decades ago. The dining room, with handmade wooden tables and chairs, is the haven in which Mrs. Mullings' Port-Antonio-famous Jamaican cooking is served. If you want to come here for a meal, call ahead for reservations for your group so that the cook has time to put the multi-course meal together.

As you wander around the rooms and upstairs halls, be sure to look at the framed pictures, which include former Jamaican Premiers Bustamante and Sangster as well as England's Queen Victoria and, in Room 7, a family picture of Queen Elizabeth and Prince Philip, when they were a family with only Charles and Anne.

There are no resort facilities here (no pool), but the beach is a reasonable drive away. The inn is within walking distance of downtown Port Antonio, a West Indian sea town that looks much as it might have when it was a turn-of-the century resort. It is best seen with the special bustle of market days.

DE MONTEVIN LODGE, Port Antonio, Jamaica. Telephone: (809) 993-2604. The 15 rooms vary as you would expect them to in a private home. All are furnished simply, but neatly, with all the basics. A few rooms have private bath; others share a bath that may be a few doors away. Room 4, with blue walls, has a balcony and private bath; Room 7, mentioned above for its picture of England's Royal Family is known as the family room and is huge. A whole family could fit in here, if the children are small. The room has a balcony and private bath.

Getting there: If you have made this a day excursion from Ocho Rios for lunch, it will take you about two hours driving east along the north coast. If you are staying for a while, the easiest route to get here is to fly from either Montego Bay or Kingston Airports on the small planes of Trans-Jamaican Airline to the airstrip at Port Antonio, west of the town. A taxi can bring you up the hill to De Montevin in about 15 minutes from the Port Antonio Airport. It's also possible to arrive in Port Antonio on one of the cruise ships.

TRIDENT VILLAS AND HOTEL, a short drive around the coast, heading southeast from the town of Port Antonio.

More luxurious than most of the places mentioned in this book, Trident qualifies because it is small and management maintains the feeling of hospitality that I feel is an integral part of innkeeping.

When you walk through the first arched doorway, you'll find the small reception room in an air-conditioned enclosure on your right. That's the most obviously businesslike part of the operation. Once you have registered and been taken to your villa, you can settle into the "private world of sun, sea and serenity" that the place touts on the front of its brochure.

An effort has been made to create a traditionally Jamaican place, even though it was built in the early 1970s. The antiques, or copies of antiques, that furnish the dining room are set off by the silver candelabra and serving pieces. Especially worth noting is the impressive meat cart on which beef is sometimes served. The silver dome is rolled back to show the dinner offering. The elegant table by the window facing the pool and the sea is set off by the straight backed chairs and two wing chairs on which you may sit to dine. (Note the grandfather clock and the other antiques that punctuate this room.)

Across the courtyard is the pub room, with its red, plush banquets and its mahogany tables that were being rubbed with marvelous smelling lemon oil when I visited recently. Oriental rugs are scattered around the polished brick floor and there's a warm feeling in this room, even when it is empty.

Peacocks saunter around the grounds, unaffected by you and other guests. They'll watch serenely as you lounge by the pool, and may follow your path to your room in one of the villas along the shore. If you want a beach, you'll have to walk or drive to one nearby. There are tennis courts on the premises.

During 1976, Trident became a member of the quality European *Relais de Campagne et Chateaux Hotels* and, even though the quality may have fluctuated slightly with the changes in management and the Jamaican political climate, you can count on finding above average fare in the dining room and in the service throughout the hotel.

This is one of the few places in Jamaica that still encourages men to wear jackets and ties for dinner. However, dressing up seems only fitting when you look at the appointments in the elegant dining room where you will have dinner by candlelight.

TRIDENT VILLAS AND HOTEL, Box 119, Port Antonio, Jamaica, W.I. Telephone: Port Antonio 993-2602 or 993-2705. The 19 "villas" are actually 8 suites and 11 studio apartments, all tastefully appointed to make the most of the white stucco walls, wood ceiling, and colorful accents. Furniture is made in Jamaica, and all rooms have those marvelous overhead fans that are more than enough to keep the temperature comfortable. The studio cottages have a bedroom with sitting area, private bath, and patio. The suites have a separate living room area, usually decorated with sisal rugs, and colorful fabrics on couches and chairs. Some rooms have air-conditioning.

Getting there: Fly first to Kingston, and then drive 2 hours to Port Antonio, or fly to Kingston or Montego Bay and take Trans-Jamaica's small plane (if the schedule is right) to the airport just west of Port Antonio. You can then take a taxi for the half hour ride to southeast of Port Antonio.

RAMPARTS INN, on a cliff overlooking the hubbub of Doctor's Cave Beach at Montego Bay.

A hideaway spot in the heart of Montego Bay's tourist confusion, Ramparts Inn is above it all—literally. The small place perches on a hillside, overlooking all the clutter that surrounds busy Doctor's Cave Beach. The shops, many other hotels, and the Jamaica Tourist Board's activities program for Doctor's Cave Beach and neighboring Cornwall Beach are right at your feet.

A traditional favorite that has survived the vagaries of Jamaica's tourist picture in recent years, Ramparts Inn offers a congenial atmosphere and is popular with people who like good value and small inn surroundings.

The food is featured, with an elaborate menu and a lot of printed praise. I thought the menu overrated on one recent visit, but have had exceptional meals here on other occasions. I would advise you to be aware of the fact that almost everything that shows the "French accent" that this inn is so proud of has to be imported—and that is not always easy. If you count on finding above average fare, you won't be disappointed. The white, stucco walls, with wood and wrought iron accents, give the dining room a Spanish air.

The thatched hut by the small pool is a pleasant place to spend some leisure hours, when the strong tropical sun that beats on you when you sit poolside gets to be too much. And when you are ready to stroll to the beach, you can brace yourself for a half mile, sunny saunter down the hill.

Dress favored for guests and staff is casual, but not sloppy.

RAMPARTS INN, Box 34, Montego Bay, Jamaica, W.I. Telephone: Montego Bay 952-4830. Most of the 17 rooms have a balcony with a sea view; all are air-conditioned. The two-story, white stucco buildings cluster around the small pool, their wooden balconies, struts, and peaked roofs helping to create the atmosphere of a small enclave. Rooms are adequately furnished, usually with two double beds, built-in vanity, small desk/table, and a private bath.

Getting there: After you have cleared customs when your plane arrives at Montego Bay, take a taxi for the 15-minute ride to Ramparts Inn.

TOBY INN, at the eastern side of the tourist hub of Montego Bay.

It may be a surprise to you, as it was to me, to find some place that's small, with a family hotel feeling at this commercial tourist center. But Toby Inn is that kind of place. Lying low at the corner of the road, where the main road bends to head inland from the sea toward the airport, Toby Inn is across the road from the big and bustling Montègo Beach Hotel. You can cross over to Montego Beach if you want more action than is offered with conversations at the Treetop Bar, *in* a tree at the heart of Toby Inn.

Rooms are motel-style, around the central reception building, but daytime activity for those who stay "at home" is poolside. The Pagoda Kai restaurant serves oriental specialities that have become popular in Jamaica in recent seasons and which are familiar to the owners/managers, the Clinton Chins, who reopened this place after extensive refurbishing in summer 1977.

If you want to find the sea for your sunning, you can walk across to the narrow strip of sand that the Montego Beach Hotel guests use, and pay a few Jamaican dollars for the privilege. Other beachside options, if you want more action, are to stroll along the shore, past an extensive array of shops specializing in gifts, straw, carved birds, and other island-made items, as well as imports at in-bond prices, and head to Cornwall Beach and Doctor's Cave Beach. Both beaches are hubs for Jamaica Tourist Board activities, beach barbecues, music nights, and all the daytime sports activities.

TOBY INN, Box 467, Montego Bay, Jamaica. Telephone: (809) 952-4370. The 26 rooms are motel-style, but clean, neat, and comfortable, offering a good value within a short walk of the MoBay action. The low (for Jamaica) rates are without meals, but you can get all meals on the premises or within walking distance at other hotels.

Getting there: Fly to Montego Bay and taxi to the hotel. The taxi fare from the nearby MoBay Airport is about J$1 and the ride will take less than 10 minutes.

SUNDOWNER, on the beach, a 10-minute drive or a leisurely hour stroll along the beach, north of the village of Negril.

When the Hojans opened Sundowner about ten years ago, they provided the only comfortable lodgings in the area. As far as I'm concerned, Rita Hojan still manages the best place at this west end of Jamaica—and, in fact, in all of Jamaica.

One of the charms of Sundowner is the hospitality that comes with a staff that has worked with Rita Hojan over the years, some of them since the inn opened. There's a family feeling. If you want to, you can become part of it; if you prefer to be left alone, that's possible also.

This inn is a place for repeaters. Many of the guests have been hiding out here for a couple of winter weeks over a period of years, and when they arrive they find few changes. Miss Hortense still reigns supreme in the kitchen, and at the head of her Sunday night buffet table. (The memory of her coconut candy and freshly baked breads and cakes makes my mouth water as I write.) And then there's Rupert who does much more than wait on tables, and Clinton, Steve, Bin, Two-bits, and the others who whisk the dishes to and fro and have been known to break into dance as they carry the trays to the kitchen. Wilton tends the thatched bar that is the hub of conversation from about noon to midnight.

Sundowner is definitely a beach-oriented place, a fact you'll quickly realize not only from the strand that stretches west to the sea and as far as the eye can see to the north and the south, but also from the simple furnishings and easily swept terrazzo floors in the rooms.

The main house that was the original inn is now the public rooms and reception area. The modern lodging rooms are in a two-story, motel-style unit to one side.

Daytime diversions are focused on the water, with a full range of sports offered by Aqua World, the concession next door. If you want to play tennis, you can walk up to Negril Beach Village to make arrangements with their tennis pro.

Evening activity begins with the sunset, best seen from a beach chair as you look out to sea. For livelier entertainment, you can dance to a band two nights a week in season, or stroll down the beach to Coconut Cove or on to the action-packed revelry of the Negril Beach Village.

SUNDOWNER, Box 5, Negril, Jamaica. Telephone: 957 4225. The 26 rooms all face the sea and, although there is air-conditioning, I've always enjoyed the sea breezes that keep the rooms cool. Each room, whether on the first floor or second, has a small terrace. I find first floor rooms preferable because you can walk right in from the beach. The highest priced rooms have a refrigerator, but all rooms are comfortable, made with terrazzo floors and furnished simply so that the beach can rule the lifestyle.

Getting there: If you've planned ahead, the hotel can send Mr. Morgan to the airport at Montego Bay to meet you. Otherwise, you will have to arrange for taxi or rental car fot the almost 2-hour ride west and south along the coast to the inn. Trans-Jamaican's small planes fly to Negril Airport from MoBay in about 15 minutes; the small Negril Airport is almsot across from the hotel.

ROCK HOUSE, perched on the rocks, at the west of the village of Negril.

Ideal for romantics, contemplative types or those with a lot of reading to do, this place is not for anyone who must have a beach within a few steps of his room. Although the surf pounds against the jagged rocks on which 10 thatched villas that make up the inn sit, there is no sandy strand in the immediate vicinity. You

109

have to make a long walk or bike ride, or a short car or taxi ride to get to the powdery sand.

Rock House is unique, and spectacular. The handful of rooms have been imaginatively constructed out of wood, with colorful fabrics to provide highlights for the sometimes austere, simple wood furnishings. Rustic elegance is the keynote, with kerosene lamps providing the night light, if you want more than the stars and the phosphorescence that you can sometimes see in the sea below.

Meals are prepared in your rooms, or in the restaurant in one of the villas—if you remember to tell the management almost 24 hours in advance. That much time allows them to prepare a memorable feast, although they can put something together on shorter notice in season. If you don't plan ahead, you are on your own to forage at nearby simple cafes and restaurants or at landmark Rick's, with one of the Caribbean's prime spots for sunset viewing. Count on seafood and local vegetables for mealtime fare.

You can dive from the rocks into the sea, and swim into and around the rocks, through caves and into pools. The area is interesting for snorkeling. It's possible to rent a bicycle in the village (but be sure to have a hat, long-sleeved shirt and plenty of sun screen lotion if you burn easily). You can walk and/or hitchhike along the road, or take a seat-in-car in one of the minibuses that ply the main beachside road, as the island folk do.

ROCK HOUSE, Box 12, Negril. Telephone: Negril (809) 957.4216. The 7 rooms are one of a kind, each with its own deck and sea view. Furnishings are rustic. The kind of wood that was used to build your cabin has been used for beds, tables, and the rest of the furnishings. Quilts and coverlets are colorful. The atmosphere is definitely "cabin-by-the-sea," thatched roof and all.

Getting there: Once you arrive at the Montego Bay Airport, you'll have to drive for almost 2 hours west along the coastal road, or, if you're lucky with the flight schedules, fly on Trans-Jamaica's small plane to the Negril Airport (a 15-minute flight).

CHARELA INN, on the beach about 10 minutes from the village of Negril.

When Charles and Pamela Mucklow opened this inn in the mid-1970s, it was to be the core of a big and extensive condominium development. I, for one, am glad that those plans have been temporarily shelved. What stands now is a lovely Spanish-style home, with a wing of rooms stretching inland. All facilities are modern because they are new but the feeling is that of an established residence.

There's the outdoor terrace or an under-cover room furnished in copies of Spanish antiques for mealtime. Both areas face the sea and beach. The beach is spectacular, not only the part in front of the inn, where you can stretch out in a lounge chair to watch the sunset, but also in the other direction, beyond the clump of mangrove trees you have to skirt to get to the action-packed Negril Beach Village, almost 3 miles down the shoreline. Brochures and public relations blurbs claim that the entire stretch is seven miles of sand, but even if it falls a couple of yards short of that, the sandy route is plenty long enough for jogging or strolling as far as you want to.

The atmosphere that the Mucklows have encouraged with their small inn is that of an island home. Dress is casual elegance, with bathing suits and cover-ups a comfortable daytime outfit. As for the food, Pamela Mucklow has put her hand to that and you'll be impressed, as I was, with the extensive menu and the pleasant Jamaican staff she has trained to serve you. (She also designed the colorful, comfortable uniform they wear.)

CHARELA INN, Box 33, Negril, Jamaica. Telephone: (809) 957-4227. The 10 rooms are all modern, furnished with two huge beds, vanity, and modern bathroom. The only drawback is that, because the

111

rooms were not placed to take advantage of the tradewinds, all must be air-conditioned. Rooms 202 and 203 are the prime spots. Both are over the dining room in the main house, with spectacular views of the sea and beach. The honeymoon suite, up the stairs at the "back" of the building, is furnished in gold and white, with a canopy bed and complete privacy.

Getting there: Brace yourself for a "long" journey. Choices include an almost 2-hour ride by taxi from Montego Bay Airport, following the coast road west, or a flight from MoBay on Trans-Jamaica to the Negril Airport and a 10-minute taxi ride to the hotel. (Trans-Jamaica's schedule may not fit yours; they seem to fly at their own convenience.)

MONTSERRAT

A neighbor of Antigua, small Montserrat has kept its 12 miles by 7 miles in cultivation since the first Irish settlers came over from nearby St. Kitts. The village of Plymouth, main town for the island, is the heart of the island's action not only on market days when the fruits and vegetables mingle with woven sisal rugs and handmade furniture, but also at other times of the day—and week. Irish place names, testimony to the effectiveness of Cromwell's purge in England, mark the maps of Montserrat and a shamrock marks the forehead of the Government House in Plymouth.

This is a quiet rural island, found by a clutch of Canadians and people from the United States who have built homes here. Small inns are the speciality of Montserrat, with one of the leaders operated by a well-known island family.

Arriving is easy on a 15-minute small plane flight that swoops into the airstrip at Montserrat from nearby Antigua.

Star attractions for people who enjoy the Caribbean's flora and fauna will be climbs to the high peaks, both of them dormant volcanoes now covered with lush tropical growth, and excursions to island coves for a swim from a black-to-silver sand beach. Montserrat is an islander's island.

Action options include hiking, scuba and snorkeling if you are experienced and have brought your own equipment (local rental is limited), and some sailing—perhaps on one of the island schooners that sails into Plymouth for market day. There is a 9-hole golf course north of Plymouth and just south of the Vue Pointe Hotel where you'll find the island's only tennis courts.

The best beach is at Carr's Bay, on the northwest coast, a good drive from most inns, or at Fox's Bay nearer Plymouth and the golf course. Rendez-vous Bay in the north, reached by boat, is one of the few white sand beaches at Montserrat.

For further information, contact the Caribbean Tourist Association, 20 East 46th Street, New York, New York 10017. Telephone: (212) 682-0435. Or write to the Montserrat Tourist Board, Box 7, Plymouth, Montserrat, W.I.

VUE POINTE HOTEL, just north of Plymouth, Montserrat, W.I.

About 25 years ago Cedric Osborne's father built the Vue Pointe. At that time it was used mostly by people who had bought land nearby and were building the vacation houses they now live in (and rent to others when they are not on the island).

The small hotel is still a gathering place for local folk and for repeat visitors, many of whom have been coming to Montserrat long enough to be considered part of the family.

The main building is the heart of activities where you go for bingo nights, movies shown under the stars, and special buffet, and barbecue nights. Highlight of the week for many is the special West Indian buffet which draws a big group of island residents.

Vue Pointe is a 10-minute drive north of the main town of Plymouth. During the day you can play tennis on one of the two tennis courts, both resurfaced in 1977 and placed so that the sun doesn't blind you or your opponents, swim at the pool at the hillside core of the hotel or at the silver sand beach, which is a short walk down to the Caribbean Sea. There is a beach hut, "The Nest," for snacks, and a new pier near the cliffs at one end of the curve for visiting yachtsmen. Belham Golf Course (9 holes along the coast) is between the hotel and the town.

The warm hospitality and good island food are due to the efforts of Cedric Osborne and his Boston-born wife, Carole. Their knowledge of island lore can send you off to explore the waterfalls with a picnic to enjoy after the forty-five minute hike from the end of the road; to climb the area around the volcano (which you can reach by an adequate road); to another nearby sandy beach, up the coast at Little Bay; or into town to enjoy the marketplace. Mini-mokes (small cars) are available at the front desk for touring ($12 per day plus gas).

VUE POINTE HOTEL, Box 65, Montserrat, West Indies. Telephone: 5210. The 12 octagonal cottages are scattered around the top of a hill that slopes down to the hotel's soft sand beach. Near the road, the main house offers dining and public rooms, with tennis courts, and pool nearby. All the rooms are comfortably, not lavishly furnished with twin beds, a sitting area, private bath, and telephone. Air conditioning is unnecessary when the louvered windows are open.

Getting there: Fly first to Antigua, to board LIAT (Leeward Islands Air Transport) for the 15-minute, small plane flight to Montserrat. From the airport a taxi ride takes you across the island, through Plymouth, and up the north coast. The journey will take about 45 minutes.

NETHERLAND ANTILLES

The six Dutch islands are in two groups: the ABC's (Aruba, Bonaire, and Curaçao) in the south, off the coast of Venezuela, and the three S's in the north (Saba, Statia as Sint Eustatius is commonly called, and Sint Maarten), between the United States Virgin Islands and Antigua. The southern three, the ABC's, are flat, sandy, and sunbaked, with few if any inns according to the definition used for this book. Most of the hotels on Aruba and Curaçao are big, highrise buildings that focus on the casinos and nightlife as much as on the sun and sea. The islands in the north, on the other hand, undulate with rolling hills, the hills of Saba being the top of a sea-wrapped volcano. While you will find big hotels on burgeoning Sint Maarten (the island shared with the French), on Saba and Statia, the only rooms are inns.

Dutch is the language, supplemented by English and the local dialect of Papiemento in the ABC's and equalled with English on the three S's; Dutch is the style of the early houses where they still exist (especially in Curaçao's Willemstad and Aruba's Oranjestad); and Dutch is the national affiliation, all six islands having firm, pre-independence links to Mother Holland.

Arrival on the ABC's is usually through Aruba or Curaçao, both with major airports and frequent daily connections to Bonaire. Sint Maarten's direct air service from New York and from Miami through San Juan is the easiest route to the three S's in the north. Cruises stop regularly at Sint Maarten's Philipsburg (for shopping) and occasionally, when the ship is small enough, drop anchor off Saba or Statia. The ABC's are ports of call on longer cruises out of Miami and island ports, especially on cruises out of Puerto Rico's San Juan.

Star attractions on the three biggest islands (Aruba, Curaçao, and Sint Maarten) are the casinos. Nightclubs supplement the tables. Shops that line the streets of the main towns (and the lobbies of big hotels) gobble the dollars you have won, or haven't wasted, the night before. Basking in the sun on island beaches is high on the list for Aruba and Sint Maarten. On Bonaire, scuba and snorkeling are the main attractions (with beaches, of course); and on Statia and Saba, visitors are calmed by quiet island life.

Action options center on the gaming tables and nightlife of the highrise hotels along Aruba's Palm Beach, on Curaçao, and on Sint Maarten. Sailors can charter on Sint Maarten for day sails to nearby Anguilla and to Saba or St. Kitts. Deep sea fishing is arranged (at a price) out of the biggest resort hotels. Scuba and snorkel enthusiasts follow the professionals to Bonaire for intensive programs; reputable firms operate from activities desks in the bigger hotels on the other islands.

There's not much in the way of golf on the sun-parched southern ABC's (unless you count the Lago course on Aruba and the Shell course on Curaçao), but Mullet Bay's course on Sint Maarten is worth the play. Tennis courts can be found at resort hotels on Aruba, Curaçao, and Sint Maarten.

Best beaches are on Aruba and Sint Maarten. The best coves on Curaçao are not at the hotels. Bonaire has beautiful beaches at quiet coves, especially on Little Bonaire, a speck in the harbor of Kralendijk. Statia's beaches are silver sand; and Saba has none.

For further information in the United States, contact the Aruba Tourist Board at 576 Fifth Avenue, New York, New York 10036. Telephone: (212) 246-3030. The Curaçao Tourist Board is at 30 Rockefeller Plaza, New York, New York 10020. Telephone: (212) 265-0230. Bonaire's Tourist Board is represented at 685 Fifth Avenue, New York, New York 10022. Telephone: (212) 838-3930. For Sint Maarten, Saba, and Sint Eustatius, contact their New York representatives at 445 Park Avenue, New York, New York 10022. Telephone: (212) 688-8350. There are on-the-spot tourist offices for Aruba at its capital of Oranjestad, Aruba, Netherlands Antilles. The Bonaire Tourist Board is at Kralendijk, Bonaire, N.A. The Curaçao Tourist Board is at Willemstad, Curaçao, N.A. The Sint Maarten Tourist Baord at Philipsburg, Sint Maarten, N.A. has information also on Saba and Sint Estatius, although each of those small islands has its own one-man office. The Saba Tourist Board is at The Bottom, Saba, N.A. The Sint Estatius Tourist Board is at Oranjestad, Sint Eustatius, N.A.

PASANGGRAHAN, Philipsburg, Sint Maarten, N.A.

For in-town convenience and a far away feeling, few places can compete with this small inn. Always popular for those who want a haven within easy walking distance of Philipsburg's shops, post office, and market, the Pasanggrahan has a following that

makes it clubby during winter months. Most of the people seem to come from New England, some from the mid-west, and all have been coming "forever." The name, by the way, means "guesthouse" in Indonesian.

The younger crowd settles in for the summer, to swim from the beach just beyond a fence that borders the gardened terrace.

The heart of the inn is small, but arrangements can be made for accommodations in the modern apartment building next door if the house count is high. In that building is one of the area's best restaurants, La Grenouille, perched on the top floor, up two flights, with a bird's eye view of the sea.

Frequent visitors prefer the oldest rooms, with their thin, wood walls, basic bathroom, and a long wooden balcony stretching in front, making it easy to meet the neighbors next door.

P4, my home on one visit, had green walls, an overhead fan, and the endless sound of the sea mingling with the noises of the town. (A late night cat fight was the subject of one day's breakfast conversation.) There was linoleum on the floor—some of the floor at least. Split bedposts affixed to the wall were the headboard.

The food is hearty, if not gourmet, served family style with no outside guests allowed in season. Pasanggrahan runs as a home-turned-inn and welcomes those who can fit into the informal, friendly atmosphere.

Everything is within easy walking distance—all the shops, markets, a long stretch of beach (that is the ribbon between harbor and the main street of town), and a handful of small spots to sip and sup.

PASANGGRAHAN, Front Street, Philipsburg, Sint Maarten, N.A. Telephone: 2388. Guests in the 24 rooms can expect an informal, simple, guesthouse atmosphere. Nightlife and several restaurants are nearby.

Getting there: Easy by taxi from the airport to Philipsburg. The fare, even with the rapidly increasing rates, should be under $5. Sint Maarten has direct flights from New York and Miami as well as convenient small plane service via San Juan, Puerto Rico and/or St. Thomas, and St. Croix in the U.S. Virgin Islands.

MARY'S BOON, between the beach and the airport runway, at Simson Bay.

If the location by the runway sounds noisy, it's worth noting that there aren't a lot of big planes (or many of any size) landing in St. Maarten. Two per day is about it, and they come in daylight hours when you are on the beach and presumably concentrating on other things than sleep. The fact is that this controversial location is typical of the unique individual who created Mary's Boon. Mary Pomeroy is Maltese, but has been in the Caribbean for long enough to be known by many as a permanent resident. My first acquaintance with her was at a delightful inn that she opened up for the few guests who could find it on rural Nevis. That place is still going, even though Mary flew away—literally—when government hassles proved too much. Since she flies her own plane, the getaway was easy. She has been back several times, however, to retrieve many of her choice antiques.

The seaside independence offered here is just what a handful of people who have discovered it (and return regularly) want most. A short walk to the front of the house brings you into an airy lobby, with the sea straight ahead. You have a choice of the lounge area (rattan furniture and louvered windows open to sea breezes) or the dining terrace, with several small tables, punctured tin cones covering overhead lights, and a dinner bell to ring for the staff—who will probably have arrived with what you want, before you pick up the bell to ring for it.

The location is ideal for the beach (and the airport), but you'll need a car or taxi for forays to other beaches and into the Dutch towns of Philipsburg or French Marigot.

MARY'S BOON HOTEL, Box 278, Philipsburg, Sint Maarten, Netherlands Antilles. Telephone: St. Maarten 4235. The 10 rooms are scattered around. Some are in the main house, upstairs over the dining room, overlooking the sea. Others are in a couple of cottages connected to the main building. All are comfortably, tropically furnished. The emphasis is on simplicity, with flourishes.

Getting there: Take a taxi from the Queen Juliana Airport and you can be in the sea within fifteen minutes, allowing time for changing your clothes. Fact is, the distance is such that you could walk over—if you were traveling light and officials permitted you to walk across the runway. The trip to either Philipsburg or Marigot, for shopping and strolling, will take about 15 minutes by car.

SIMSON BAY BEACH HOTEL, Simson Bay, Sint Maarten, N.A.

Great fanfare greeted the opening of this 20-room hotel several years ago. It was intended to be the start of a bigger resort right on the beach (a pretty white sand one, at that), just off the road from the airport into Philipsburg on the Dutch side of this dual-nationality island. The big opening led only to a big closing. For the past few seasons, the property had been a down-at-the-heels nightclub and quarters for the help from nearby hotels.

But all of that is now changed. Experienced hotelier Ron Mulder, former manager of the Caravanserai Hotel, took over the property in early 1977 and his ability as an innkeeper has put everything in top order. Gourmet dining at the attractive al fresco area at the edge of the beach is pleasant by starlight, casual and comfortable at midday.

The rooms are in two- and three-story units, sharing walls but appearing to be independent. Construction is Mediterranean-style, which gives the inn the look of a small village.

One of the pleasantest memories of my first stay was the chance to be up and in the sea before breakfast. That is still one of the great attractions, as well as the opportunity for sailing on the lagoon across the road or snorkeling in the sea off the beach in front of the hotel.

You'll find informality with class. A car is not necessary, but can be helpful for at least a day if you want to tour the island or get into the free port shops that line the two main streets and several cross-streets of Dutch Philipsburg, and the French side's main town of Marigot.

SIMSON BAY BEACH HOTEL, Simson Bay, Sint Maarten, N.A. Telephone: 4279. 20 modern, double rooms. Ten minutes from the airport and, continuing on the same road, about ten minutes from Philipsburg, capital of the Dutch part of the island. Casual, comfortable, a lazy kind of place with lots of opportunity for lolling on the beach and snorkeling.

Getting there: Take a taxi for the 5-minute ride from Queen Juliana Airport, after a nonstop flight on KLM or American from New York or Miami. Connecting flights come from Puerto Rico (Prinair) or the U.S. Virgins.

OYSTER POND YACHT CLUB, on a seaside rise with a beautiful view of the Caribbean and St. Barths, about a 20-minute drive from Philipsburg.

Built to cater to a select clientele, the Club has never been lively when I've seen it, but when there's a congenial crowd in the middle of high season, I'm sure it can be. It's picture perfect: a cluster of white stucco planes and angles, red tile roofs, and an interior that emphasizes nautical antiques, with binacles and compasses on tables, and yacht club flags trimming the edge of the open-to-the-breezes lobby.

121

You enter through the flag room, decorated with campaign chests and antique furniture. Around the center courtyard, open to the sky, there are stairways to the second floor rooms. The dining room and the lounge, both face the sea. Food in the dining room has been exceptionally good everytime I have been here, especially in the evening. (For lunch, I prefer some of the seaside fish places in Marigot, the French side capital, or in nearby Grand Case, also on the French side and about a ten-minute drive from the Oyster Pond Yacht Club.

There's a path that leads to the beach, and an outdoor area for al fresco dining, accompanied with barbecue flourishes on some evenings in season. The water sports facilities are across the road and parking area, bordering a lagoon which is fitted out to be a marina, although only a few boats seem to have found it.

This is a leisurely inn, with class. The liveliest entertainment can be found by driving into Philipsburg (Dutch side), or touring the French part of the island in your rental car. (Many of the inn's earlier guests have bought land and built the big houses that you see on the hillside just inland from your perch.)

A comment from the guest book, soon after the place opened, added to the host of laudatory comments ("beautiful," "heavenly," "love it") was that it is "worth risking your life for the drive in." That has changed now with paved roads, but The Club is certainly out of the mainstream, a point in its favor for many.

OYSTER POND YACHT CLUB, Box 239, Philipsburg, Sint Maarten, Netherlands Antilles. Telephone: St. Maarten 2206. The 20 rooms vary, and so does the view, but all are attractive. After your first visit, you'll have a favorite. There is a tower studio available for four people. Room 6 has red, white, and blue decor. Rooms M, N, O, and P look out over the Caribbean; others face the harbor/lagoon. In many of the rooms, you can sit on the balcony and watch pelicans dive. That may be your main amusement.

Getting there: By car, from Queen Juliana Airport, it will take you about 45 minutes—with the last part a twisting, bumpy route. Signposts leave a lot to be desired, so if you're driving yourself the first time, be sure to ask directions—and then look for the arrowless sign which indicates (now that you've been told) where you should turn right to get to the Club.

MOOSHAY BAY PUBLICK HOUSE, across the narrow road at Lower Town, on the inland side of The Old Gin House.

The frame of this inn is one of the old stone buildings that stood at the shore when the town was in its 18th century heyday. The interior is completely modern, but done in the old style except for the conveniences. It's decorated with the same good taste—antiques mixed with practical furnishings—that has made the Old Gin House a place to which you want to return.

Delft and pewter recall the Dutch past of the island, and the appointments in the dining area are a pleasure to look at while you wait for your meal to be served.

There is a small pool in what was formerly the cistern, used to gather rainwater for the fresh water supply, and all the facilities of the Old Gin House are only a few steps away. Although some guests prefer to be "separate-but-equal," most mingle with visitors at the sister resort across the road. That makes for a larger crowd and a friendly, house-party atmosphere.

No matter where you stay, unless you are an owl by nature or get hooked into a backgammon game, bed and wakeup times will be early.

THE MOOSHAY BAY PUBLICK HOUSE, St. Eustatius, Nether-
lands Antilles. Telephone: St. Eustatius 03-2319. The 14 rooms are
all new (the place opened in late 1976), with modern baths and
overhead fans (air conditioning is unnecessary with trade winds
and the fans).

Getting there: Take a taxi from the Statia Airport for the
15-minute ride. You'll have arrived at Statia via Winair from
St. Maarten (12-minute flight). If you come by sail, you can
anchor offshore and swim in.

THE OLD GIN HOUSE, at the water's edge where the Lower
Town used to be, and a short walk down from the Upper Town
of Oranjestad.

When John May and Marty Scofield left the rigors of
northeastern winters to open this inn a few years ago, they
started out with the restaurant. It was then about the only place
for a good meal, and certainly the only one beside the water. The
few guest rooms came later, in response to visitors who flew over
for the day from nearby St. Maarten and wanted to stay on for an
extra day or two.

Although the atmosphere is primarily geared to relaxation,
there are things to do here things as strenuous as walking along
the silver sand beach that runs along the shoreline, a few steps
off the terrace, or climbing the slope to Upper Town to browse
through the small library. You can climb Mount Mazinga or
venture into The Quill, a dormant volcano's crater, now dense
with tropical growth and land crabs which Statians catch and
cook for dinner.

Nightlife will be as lively as the guests; dinner will be by
candlelight; and dinner music will be gentle conversation and
the swish of waves on the shore at your feet.

Furnishings are island and other antiques, or copies of same,
pleasantly adorned with flowered fabric. Mosquito-netting
hangs over the four-poster beds, if you need it. The inn is open to
the breezes. They (and it) are close to perfection.

THE OLD GIN HOUSE, St. Eustatius, Netherlands Antilles.
Telephone: St. Eustatius 03-2319. There are 11 rooms; eight in a
two-story unit on the sea (the upper rooms have a slightly better

view but both upper and lower are attractively furnished.) The other three rooms are in the courtyard, set back from the seaside terrace and the small bar.

Getting there: Same as for Mooshay Bay: a taxi for the 15-minute ride to town and down to the shore, after you've taken the 12-minute Winair flight from St. Maarten.

CAPTAIN'S QUARTERS, in the village of Windwardside about 1,900 feet above sea level.

When you get to know this place well, you may tire as I have, of all the references to "story book village" and "botanist's paradise," and the talk of the village called The Bottom being "in the bottom of a volcanic crater" (which, in fact, it is not, it is in a valley). However, if you've never heard of Saba, all those phrases will help you picture this very special island, the tip of a mountain that pokes out of the Caribbean to perch on the horizon as you look south from Sint Maarten.

The inn known as Captain's Quarters is a perfectly trimmed-up Saban cottage which the management claims was a sea captain's lodging. Since most of the Sabans are sea folk, no one will contest that claim. Most of the people who find their way to the island will also find their way to Captain's Quarters, if not for overnight, then at least for lunch.

Today's visitors are an eclectic lot, some of whom are content to curl up by the speck of a pool with a book in hand, others of whom want to undertake the island's most strenuous activity—a climb up the 1,000-plus stone steps from the village to the heights of Mount Scenery, with its verdant botanic-garden cap, and veil of mist. Saba has no beach—and very few tourists.

Captain's Quarters punctuates its authentic building with authentic antiques, some from the island or neighboring islands and others imported from Europe and the States. The four-posters in the bedrooms are island pieces, and there are 18th century wig stands that add to the atmosphere in some rooms.

Whether you choose to sit around the comfortable common rooms on the main floor, around the pool, or in your room, you will definitely feel that you are a part of island life when you settle into the Captain's Quarters. Everyone who is anyone stops in here at least long enough for a Saban Spice.

CAPTAIN'S QUARTERS, Saba, Netherlands Antilles, Cable address: CAPQUA. (There is no telephone.) The 10 rooms in the main house are airy and comfortably furnished with antiques. They vary in size, as you'd expect in a small home, and are some of the few island facilities with hot and cold running water. A separate building, Bessie's Cottage, has two double rooms, one single room, 2 baths, and a sitting room, and is available for week-long or longer rental.

Getting there: The first step is to fly to Sint Maarten. From that island, you can take the small Winair plane, a STOL (Short take-off and landing) plane, for the 15-minute flight to Saba's 1250-foot airstrip, or you can arrive by boat, on a small-boat cruise from Sint Maarten. Boat arrivals come ashore at the pier at Fort Bay.

SCOUT'S PLACE, in the village of Windwardside, up the mountainside from Hell's Gate and about 2000 feet from the top of Mount Scenery.

When I first came to Saba, this place offered the only overnight accommodations for the public. It was known as the Government Guest House, sometimes called Windwardside Guest House and, although the building was typical of the others in town with its wood fretwork and other trimmings neatly embellishing the basic, square box construction, the place had promise even then.

Given the imagination and flair of one-time Ohio resident Scout Thirkield, the place has come into its own, with an individuality that takes its spark from the owner. Scout arrived in Sint Maarten in the early days of that island's tourism and had been involved with two properties there, the Pasanggrahan Guest House (which still looks pretty much the same as it did in the early 1950s) and the Caravanserai (which has yielded some of its early special character to commercial tourism). In the late 1960s, when tourism threatened to tromp with a heavy foot on Sint Maarten, Scout took off for Saba where he managed Captain's Quarters for six years.

In 1973, Scout opened his own place by taking over and putting his touches on the old Windwardside Guest House. The only "advertising" that Scout does—other than word of mouth from satisfied visitors—is a card that says "Scout's Place. Bed'n' Board. Cheap'n'Cheerful. Saba, Netherlands Antilles." The card I first saw (and still keep) makes the claim in black ink on day-glow yellow-green. That is by far the most startling aspect of the place, other than an occasional guest's behavior.

The inn is small, very simple, and certainly not for fussy types. Food is satisfactory, if not gourmet, and the rooms are adequate, but don't count on hot running water. Cold water is available, but the sun tends to make all water tepid.

SCOUT'S PLACE, Windwardside, Saba, Netherlands Antilles. Cable address: SCOUT SABA NA. (There is no telephone.) All meals are included in your rate when you make reservations for one of Scout's 4 rooms. You can count on simple, imaginative furnishings in your room and, while Scout's Place may not be the most lavish inn you've ever stayed in, you'll find plenty of outpost-island atmosphere.

Getting there: From Sint Maarten, your arrival will be either at the airstrip aboard one of the small Winair planes that makes the flight between Sint Maarten's Juliana Airport and the airstrip in Saba in about 15 minutes, or by sea to Fort Bay Pier, where a taxi can take you to Windwardside. From the airfield or Fort Bay, the drive wiggles through the village of Hell's Gate and on up the mountainside to the sort of plateau that is Windwardside.

PUERTO RICO

The tropical forest on the sides of El Yunque, the phosphorescent bay at the south coast near Parguera, the fishing villages at the east end, the Taino Indian ballpark in the midlands in the western half of the island, and the coffee plantations and the rural life often get lost in the minds of most travelers amid the swirl of the casino wheels and the blazing neon lights of the San Juan-Condado area. More's the pity. The 100 mile by 35 mile rectangular shape of Puerto Rico offers some of the Caribbean's most interesting scenery, and some of the best off-beat touring possibilities.

Still a Commonwealth of the United States, although the present Governor, elected to his office in 1976, is staunchly for statehood, Puerto Rico's natural features are decidedly Spanish. The language of the country is Spanish, although you will find most people involved with visitors are also fluent in English. Old time customs prevail in the mid-island villages, and the restoration in the city of Old San Juan is a pace-setter for the Caribbean (and the model for the recent restoration of the Dominican Republic's capital of Santo Domingo). The authentic refurbishing of Casa Blanca (the house of Ponce de Leon), of Forteleza where the ruler of Puerto Rico has lived since settlement soon after discovery by Columbus (and where the Governor now resides), and the museums, shops, and restaurants that fill the restored 16th, 17th, and 18th century buildings make the Old San Juan area an intriguing place to stroll.

Arriving is easy via nonstop flights from major United States cities on American Airlines, Eastern or Delta. Week-long cruises out of Miami include Puerto Rico's San Juan; several smaller cruise ships use San Juan as a departure port for fly/cruise travel to the islands to the east and south.

Star attractions are the casinos and nightlife for some folk, but people interested in island history, flora, and fauna will get out of the hubbub around San Juan and head for the hills. The highrise havens are in the San Juan-Condado area, but there are resort hubs east of San Juan on the north coast and at Fajardo, southeast near Humacao, near Ponce (Puerto Rico's second city) on the south coast, at Mayaguez on the west coast and at the town of Dorado west of San Juan on the north coast. The Paradores Puertorriqueños, a chain of inns patterned after the successful paradores project in Spain, are government-assisted, family-operated small hotels with traditions. Unique in the group are Baños de Coamo, refurbished from an island spa popular in the 1800s; Gripiñas, with tin-roof, rockers on the veranda, tropical gardens, and a waterfall at a former coffee plantation at Jayuya; and the Casa del Frances on the island of Vieques, built as an island home for a French planter who wanted some place more remote than his plantation in the French West Indies.

Action options are endless. If you have the stamina, you can keep going 24 hours a day, ending with a swim when the casinos finally close in the early hours of the morning. At beaches near resorts, and certainly along the Condado-San Juan shore, you'll find a full range of watersports, including waterskiing, deep sea fishing (with boats leaving from nearby harbors to head out to sea), scuba and snorkeling (usually at waters away from the string of hotels). Tennis is the focus at Dorado Hotels, at Palmas del Mar near Humacao and at the Carib Inn and other hotels near San Juan; golfers head for Dorado, El Conquistador, Palmas del Mar, Rio del Mar and the course at Punta Boriquen.

Evening extravaganzas can be found at the Condado-San Juan highrise hotels and there are government-controlled casinos at most big resorts, in addition to the race track at Commandante for those who want to play the horses. Small bars and bistros fill the streets of Old San Juan and Puerto Rico's own LeLoLai Festival includes traditional island parties with a Jibara beach buffet, the Areyto Folkloric Ballet and African bomba drummers offering a weekly program. Symphonies, concerts, and art exhibitions are held in historic buildings, with the highlight of that activity being the annual Pablo Casals Festival in late May.

Best beaches are out of the San Juan area, although there is a narrow strand with plenty of activity along the sea in front of the highrise hotels. Luquillo public beach, east of San Juan on the north coast, is a popular beach, and there are sandy coves on most shores. Surf rolls in at the west end's Rincon area. Count on going to the offshore islands of Vieques, Culebra and the uninhabited islands and cays off the east end if you want long stretches of powdery sand.

For further information, contact the Puerto Rico Tourist Information Office, 1290 Avenue of the Americas, New York,

New York 10019. Telephone: (212) 541-6630. When you arrive in Puerto Rico, you will find efficient and well-staffed offices for visitor inquiries at the aALript near the main baggage claim area and at the cruise ship pier in Old San Juan.

EL CANARIO, on Ashford Avenue, in the Condado section of Puerto Rico, not far from downtown San Juan.

Almost in the shadow of the towering, beachside Sheraton, this small former home quietly goes about its guest house business leaving guests free to enjoy as much or as little of the surrounding casinos and cabarets as each wants. El Canario is a simple spot, with adequate rooms (nothing lavish) and a congenial, casual atmosphere. There's a pool at the back of the house (on the side toward the beach), but many guests prefer walking down the sidewalk toward the Sheraton to that long stretch of sand, with all its bustle and hot dog stands.

If you don't care about having a big, air-conditioned room, this place offers a good value—a convient location in the middle of Puerto Rico's action. You can stroll to the shops, to the big hotels, and to the bus for the trip into Old San Juan or out around the island. Run by a couple who do their best to make your stay easy and comfortable, El Canario is fine for an overnight stay in this area—but there will be noise. Most of the action for which Puerto Rico is famous is all around you.

EL CANARIO, 1317 Ashford Avenue, Condado area, Puerto Rico. Telephone: (809) 724-2793. Don't expect anything lavish. You'll have basic comforts and hospitable surroundings when you stay in one of the 20 air-conditioned rooms. Continental breakfast is included in the reasonable rates.

Getting there: Taxi from the San Juan Airport will take you about 20 minutes, depending on traffic and the confusion of one way streets. You can get to the historic and shopping section of Old San Juan by public bus or by taxi, in about 25 minutes—again, depending on traffic.

BAÑOS DE COAMO, Coamo, Puerto Rico.

I first saw Baños de Coamo before it had officially opened as one of the chain of government-sponsored paradores. Although the recent (and frequent) rains in this part of the mountains had made the grounds a sea of mud, the place was still magnificent. A subsequent visit, after the official opening, proved that the dream of Baños de Coamo was worth all the effort—and plenty of effort was involved.

Baños de Coamo was one of Puerto Rico's earliest resorts, having opened in 1853 when visitors had to travel at least four hours on horseback to reach it. Hot springs were the prime lure in the early days, but now it is the restful countryside with the Puerto Rican coqui (the small tree frogs that chirp most of the time) and masses of brilliant flowers that make Banos de Coamo an ideal haven for botanists and those in search of peace and quiet.

The main building, where the restaurant and sitting area are located, has been painstakingly restored to preserve its decorative doorways and interesting lines. The hot spring baths are next to the central building.

The 19th century architecture of the houses around the small plaza of the town of Coamo are worth a look. Note the Catholic church which dates from 1579, the year the town was settled.

For diversion, set aside a day for the 20-mile drive to Ponce's spectacular art museum. In a building designed by Edward Durrell Stone, this modern museum holds treasures assembled by former governor, Luis Ferre, the museum's main sponsor, as well as changing exhibits of contemporary Puerto Rican art.

Ponce's Plaza Degatu, with its huge white cathedral and ornate lamp posts and fountains, is impressive and photogenic. The weirdly painted firehouse mentioned by everyone (and now I, too, have succumbed), isn't worth much more than a glance. It's too "pop art" for my taste, but you may find it charming.

After a day in town, it's fun to head for El Tuque, a beach just outside the city off Highway 2, for the best sea swimming in the area. Baños de Coamo has spa baths for a late afternoon refresher when you return to your hotel.

BAÑOS DE COAMO, Coamo, Puerto Rico 00640. Telephone: not available. In the mountains, inland on the south coast. The 48 rooms are in two-storied, traditional style buildings around a center courtyard filled with a tropical garden and a huge old tree. All rooms are modern, having been built and tiled in late 1976. Horseback riding and spa baths are the main entertainment. Beaches are a 14-mile drive down mountain roads to the south shore.

Getting there: Head out from San Juan in a rented car on Route 1 to Caguas and Cayey. At Cayey, continue south through the tobacco growing country on Route 14 to Coamo. The drive takes a good hour.

PARADOR GUAJATACA, near Quebradillas, Puerto Rico.

It was about four in the afternoon when Senora Chavez brought out the first empanada, a meat-filled tart, hot from the oven and cooked according to the family recipe. Most of her guests had already had lunch, but this was my first visit to Parador Guajataca (the name means "ocean breeze") and sampling some of the food for which the place is famous was one reason for my visit.

Guajataca has been in the Chavez family for at least two generations. The first small inn was the home of Senor Chavez's parents. Their own hospitality—and the excellent local cooking—brought guests to sit under a tree next to the house to enjoy the sea breezes that waft across the blufftop on which the new hotel now stands.

The core of the present Guajataca is on the site of the house, but that's about all that remains of the original building. Even the present 38-room inn is quite different from what I saw three years ago on my first visit. Only the hospitality of the Chavez family has not changed—and their home-cooked Puerto Rican foods.

The 38 motel-style rooms are clean, neat, and simple, if suffering somewhat from that same sea breeze that makes life here so pleasant. Unfortunately stucco and fresh paint are hard to keep free of mildew in moist shoreside climates—and the Chavez family knows that well!

The inn is still a popular gathering place for the local folk, especially for weddings and celebrations from families in the Quebradillas area. The pool is popular in summer months—but you can have it pretty much to yourself mid-week and in winter (when most Caribbean folk find it "too cold"—at an average temperature of 75°—to swim!).

The air-conditioned lounge area is not as pleasant, for my money, as the open-air poolside area overlooking the sea — or even as a stroll along the beach when the wind is less than its usual strong.

The nearby town of Quebradillas, which celebrated its 300th anniversary in 1975, is a surprise to those who have only seen San Juan. Elaborate, "gingerbread" fretwork decorates the main buildings in the town, and work goes on as usual in this country village at Puerto Rico's northeast coast.

PARADOR GUAJATACA, Quebradillas, Puerto Rico 00742. Telephone: (809) 895-3970. The 38 rooms are in a motel-style, two-story unit that stretches along the blufftop parallel to the sea. Views are excellent from all rooms when the spray doesn't cloud the glass. All rooms have private bath and comfortable, if not lavish, furnishings. The place is very popular with families — both local and visiting (Puerto Rican, Canadian, and people from the U.S.).

Getting there: Driving is the only way. From the San Juan area it takes almost four hours along Route 2, the north shore road. Taking a plane from San Juan to Mayaguez and driving from there brings the trip to half-an-hour flying time, plus about one hour from the airport following Route 2 north and east to Guajataca.

HACIENDA GRIPINAS, on a coffee plantation in the mountains almost at the center of the island of Puerto Rico.

The meal I munched on while Juan Cosme was talking about the plans for Gripinas was thoroughly Puerto Rican fare. It was my lunch, but should have been dinner for two. The menu was made for the farm folk who live in this area, and for the many Puerto Rican families who head out here on weekends for what has become a traditional Sunday buffet, when as many as 200 people enjoy the outing.

At all other times, Hacienda Gripiñas is peaceful, quiet, and buried in the coffee country. I had seen the property first when the tin roof was rusted and collapsing, when the vines and verdant tropical growth threatened to strangle the house at its heart, and when a lot of imagination — mine and, more importantly, that of the principals who were then running the Puerto

Rican Development Company—was required to picture the inn as it is today.

Guajataca, the first of the government-assisted inns called paradores, had just opened and Gripiñas was to be next. It showed promise then—and proved to be true to the promise on subsequent visits.

The house was originally part of a coffee plantation, built in the prosperous days of the 1850s when the plantation at Jayuya issued its own coins and was a self-sufficient economic community. Coffee plantation workers were paid in coin which they then used for their necessities, bought at the company store.

Today, the staff of Gripiñas comes from the neighborhood. When 30-year-old former school teacher Juan Cosme was the manager of the property, he planned to keep it local. He had lived in the town all his life, and knew the area's traditions.

The main rooms of the home-turned-inn are filled with Puerto Rican country furniture. Wood and wicker rockers are in the open-air living room and on the verandah where you can enjoy a glorious view of the valley, the mountains beyond and the remnants of the plantation's buildings below. When it rains, you can meditate to the tune of torrents on a tin roof. At other times, you can do as a violinist from Puerto Rico's Casals Festival did: bring your tape recorder and symphony tapes and listen to them while you ponder on the porch.

This is not a sand-and-sea inn; it is settled in the hills of Puerto Rico where the tempo is set by the coqui, the small tree frog that will chirp incessantly as soon as the sun starts to go down. There are opportunities for horseback riding, for swimming in the pool into which a waterfall cascades, and to wander around the verdant hillsides inspecting the tropical plants.

HACIENDA GRIPIÑAS, Route 527, Jayuya, Puerto Rico. Telephone: (809) 763-8855. Each of the 9 rooms is different, as you would expect in a home-turned inn. My favorite is up the stairs off the dining area, with a view of the hillside from its small window. All rooms have sisal rugs on the floor and an open-air, simple hospitality helped along by the handmade Puerto Rican decorations.

Getting there: If you rent a car, be sure to get a map. You have a choice of either: 1) Heading west from San Juan along Route 2 to Arecibo and then south on Route 10 to Utuado to turn south east on wiggly Route 111 to follow that road through route number changes to Jayuya where you turn south onto 527 to the Hacienda; or 2) Head south from the airport on the new highway to Ponce (about 80 miles, 128 km) on the south coast, and then go north on Route 10 to branch northeast on 140, then north on 140 to wiggle along until you connect with 144 and are at Jayuya to connect with 527. The drive takes about 1½ hours. Another option is to take a taxi from the International Airport, but then you are without a rental car and tied to the inn.

HACIENDA JUANITA, Maricao, Puerto Rico.

One of the Puerto Rican government-sanctioned chain of country inns, Hacienda Juanita is a former coffee plantation and quite different from the traditional beach and sun atmosphere one expects on Caribbean islands.

The winding and verdant route to Maricao weaves through some of the most gorgeous parts of the countryside, past small rural villages. When you arrive, you'll think you are miles from everywhere, but the hubbub of Mayaguez, Puerto Rico's western city with its Hilton Hotel, is only 12 miles away. I wandered around the grounds of the Hacienda Juanita just prior to its official opening in late 1976 and was impressed with the efforts that had been made to keep the place traditional country Puerto Rican.

The new rooms, near the former plantation house where the central facilities are located, have completely modern facilities, including tiled bathrooms.

Fresh mountain breezes keep the temperature cool, even cold in the evening, and Puerto Rico's small tree frog, the coqui, chirps incessantly. There's a dining room with an outdoor terrace and a lounge area that is conducive to relaxed conversation or quiet meditation.

Tucked into a mountain pocket, the parador is not far from forest preserves, the Monte del Estado picnic and recreation area, and the contrasting countryside of the south, where there are arid areas with cactus and huge stretches of salt flats, where water sits to be sun dried leaving a layer of salt to be scraped off and sold. For a day's tour head for La Parguera to look at the phosphorescent bay and to swim at the government-operated beach at Boqueron.

Facilities at Hacienda Juanita are scheduled for expansion. The former workers' quarters will eventually be replaced with modern guest rooms built in the old style.

The smell of coffee was strong, coming in with the breezes. Although the main building of the plantation has been modernized as the heart of the parador, coffee grinding and roasting still goes on. Coffee bushes cover the slopes around the Hacienda and a stroll down Company Street, the main working area, recalls a past prosperity, which may well return with today's coffee prices!

HACIENDA JUANITA, Maricao, Puerto Rico 00706. Telephone: not available. The 11 room inn on a former coffee plantation has all modern rooms, but the feeling is traditional. This is not the typical Caribbean of sun and sea. In fact, the beach at Boqueron is about 40 minutes away, but for peace and quiet in the mountains, for recollecting, and for reading, Hacienda Juanita offers much. Puerto Rican food is served. Horseback riding and mountain walks are easily arranged. A rental car is advisable for mobility.

Getting there: The drive from San Juan's airport takes about two hours, south on the new highway and west along the Ruta Panoramica (Route 143). A faster way to get there is to fly Prinair from San Juan International Airport to Mayaguez, then rent a car for the drive into the mountains on Route 105 to Maricao.

CASA DEL FRANCES, Esperanza on Vieques Island, Puerto Rico.
Under former management, Casa del Frances was always simple and occasionally slack in its management. Once known as the Sportsman's House, and very casual, the inn has now come into its own. Owners, American Paul Caron and his French wife, are not in residence full time (they also live in Brussels), but the inn is operated by a member of the family who shares their love of simple-but-special island life. Entertainment focuses on a congenial group of guests and the great outdoors, including horseback riding.

A brochure describing Casa del Frances in a past incarnation listed the entertainment as "loafing and sunset watching." Both are still important, but a trip by boat to Puerto Mosquito at nightfall on a moonless night is also well worth the effort. The phosphorescence sparkles as you move across the black water, rivaling the stars overhead.

The inn tops a hill overlooking the south shore, within a short distance of three powdery white sand beaches. Built in the early 1900s by a man from the French West Indies, it is a retreat of open air breezeways and rooms with high ceilings and overhead fans. Doors open into a center courtyard where trees and shrubs flourish. Nearby there's a small pool.

On the cove of Sun Bay, near Casa del Frances, the

137

government has constructed minimal beach facilities. The beach is about a mile long and palm-fringed. Snorkeling, scuba diving, and all water sports are available, but don't count on fancy or elaborate equipment.

The main town of Isabela Segunda, not much to look at but the only thing there is in the way of "city" life, is about four miles away. This resort is a quiet place to relax and enjoy the good life.

The island's population of about 800 people is rural for the most part. Farming and fishing are the main occupations.

CASA DEL FRANCES, Esperanza, Vieques, Puerto Rico 00765. Telephone: (809) 741-3751. The 16-room inn is one of the group of Paradores Puertorriqueños, which means quality service and clean, neat accommodations. Rooms are simple and the place is ideal for a casual, outdoor holiday.

Getting there: The easiest route is to fly Vieques Air Link or Culebra de Aviacion from San Juan Airport, a trip of about 45 minutes aboard a small plane. The plane lands on a strip about a 15-minute drive from Esperanza, a short drive from Casa del Frances. There's also boat service aboard the government ferry operating out of the east end of the town of Fajardo; but the channel crossing is ROUGH and I don't recommend the boat unless you like rugged travel. Fajardo is about an hour and a half's drive from Isla Grande Airport.

ST. KITTS and NEVIS

Sir Thomas Warner was one of the first overnight visitors on St. Kitts, when he arrived with his wife, his son, and a small group of settlers in 1623. And Alexander Hamilton who was born there and Admiral Horatio Nelson who married Fanny Nisbet there are the names to know for Nevis.

The two islands are joined as one Associated State of England, a status granted in 1967 when, along with the island of Anguilla which has since pulled off on its own, preliminary steps were taken toward eventual independence. The present government of St. Kitts-Nevis has wisely opted to encourage the traditional source of income—agriculture. Adding the new crop of peanuts to the traditional crop of sugar, the country has gradually moved from a plantocracy with absentee ownership of huge tracts of land to a system of land grants tilled by the local folk on behalf of their government cooperatives.

Visitors will see rolling, cane-covered hills on St. Kitts, with the ruins of the fort at Brimstone Hill an impressive sight to see on the east coast. (The offical, but seldom used, name for St. Kitts is St. Christopher, and that is the name you will see on the postage stamps.) Nevis rises five miles off the south shore of St. Kitts, and is a place time forgot. Verdant hillsides are a tangle of growth. The shore-rimming road leads you to the island's inns, but hiking into the interior or riding horseback over inland trails will add a new angle to your holiday.

Arriving on St. Kitts is an island-hopping adventure, via Prinair or LIAT from St. Maarten, St. Croix, or Antigua. It is possible to charter a plane in Puerto Rico, or in Antigua, for faster service. To reach Nevis, you have a choice of Eastern Caribbean Airways from St. Croix, flights from Antigua or St. Kitts, or the daily boat service that connects the Kittitian capital of Basseterre to Charlestown, the main town of Nevis.

Star attractions for these two islands are natural ones, the result of centuries of gradual growth and the fact that both specks are out of the tourism mainstream. Although you will find basic conveniences at the inns, many of which had been private homes in plantation days, there will be little in the way of elaborate, planned entertainment. On St. Kitts, you can prowl

Brimstone Hill, perched on its limestone clifftop from which you can overlook a spectacular Caribbean view. On Nevis, the town of Charlestown is for strolling. It comes to life when the boat from St. Kitts docks, and slumbers the rest of the time.

Action options for St. Kitts can include a day of fishing if you contact Colin Pereira at his Ocean Terrace Inn; a sail on the trimaran owned by Philip Walwyn at Rawlins Plantation; a round of golf on the course that spans the island at Frigate Bay, south of Basseterre; and perhaps a game of tennis on one of a handful of island courts. Otherwise your activity will be limited to conversations with the local fisherman and the vegetable women in the town market. On Nevis, most people head for the beaches when they tire of reading a book or walking an island path. Tennis is possible at a couple of the island inns; otherwise content yourself with a game of darts.

Best beaches are on the south coast of St. Kitts (reached only by boat) and at coves on Nevis. There's a nice patch of sand at Nisbet Plantation, and another just outside Charlestown at Pinney's Beach.

For further information, contact the Caribbean Tourism Association, 20 East 46th Street, New York, New York 10017. Telephone: (212) 682-0435. On St. Kitts, there is a Tourist Office at the pier in Basseterre, St. Kitts, West Indies. (25¢ postage per half-ounce airmail.)

BANANA BAY, on the south shore of St. Kitts, a boat ride down the coast from the capital of Basseterre.

This is Mrs. Schmidt's place, over a rise in the terrain from The Cockleshell, and on a neighboring bay. It is possible to walk from one place to the other, but it's not encouraged by either management. The same adventuresome spirit that lured both Mrs. Schmidt and the Bowers to this hard-to-get-to end of the island makes each one of them want to believe that they are the only ones who made it—successfully.

There's a white, sandy beach on which you will spend your days, unless you go boating to Nevis which you can clearly see across the channel as you munch your breakfast and plan your day. In her attractive, handwritten folder, Mrs. Schmidt says that "Banana Bay attracts the like-minded few. The idea is to relax and be yourself and our plan is to help you slip into casual island ways as easily as did the buccaneers and the beachcombers of old." The only problem is that you will see very few, if any, other people and certainly see nothing of the life of St. Kitts as the Kittitian knows it.

You can swim, snorkel and, if you've brought your own equipment and are experienced, scuba dive in almost virgin waters.

BANANA BAY BEACH HOTEL, Box 188, St. Kitts, West Indies. Cable address: BANANABAY STKITTS. (There is no telephone.) There are 10 rooms, all of them built from cement and wood fairly recently. All have modern plumbing and comforts, but nothing lavish. Life is simple; clothes should be also.

Getting there: Fly to St. Kitts from San Juan, Puerto Rico, or from Sint Maarten or from St. Croix in the United States Virgin Islands. Once at the airport, take a taxi to Basseterre for a boat to Banana Bay if that is how they have advised you to arrive.

THE COCKLESHELL, on the south coast of St. Kitts, looking across the channel to the sister island of Nevis.

I had known of The Cockleshell long before I first saw it. Bill and Georgie Bowers are staunch supporters of the Caribbean Hotel Association—and I am a staunch supporter of the Bowers, especially after my first visit to Cockleshell.

British-born Bill Bowers had just come out of a hospital in the United States when he welcomed me aboard his motor boat for the coast-cuddling route south and east out of the Kittitian capital of Basseterre. His effervescent personality had not changed a bit in light of his operation, and he clambered around the boat, hefting the produce and essential supplies that had been picked up in Basseterre along with me. (Boat-and-sea is the only route for both produce and guests to get to the inn; there is no passable overland route.)

When the boat was beached to put me ashore on the powdery sand that stretches from the Caribbean to the cottages, Georgie came to the shore to lend a hand. Although she hadn't expected me, the welcome was warm and I had a full tour of the facilities, plus a look at the library (where I found a book I wanted to borrow) and some time to talk with the fortunate guests.

This is no place for peripatetic types who must be near

phone and the means for a quick exit. You are isolated—
blissfully and completely. Robinson Crusoe never had it so
good. Thanks to the Bowers, all comforts are here. The rooms are
square, cement blocks, but colorful fabric dresses them up, and
after all, you're here to enjoy the beach and the sun, and maybe
to play on the cement slab that passes for a tennis court. (It's not
worth bringing your racket, but the Bowers have some you can
borrow.)

This is a home-turned-inn and, once you get here, you
won't want to leave. (And when you do leave, it may be that the
boat trip across the channel to the island of Nevis, where a taxi
can take you to that airstrip will be an easier way out than the
longer and sometimes rougher ride up the coast to St. Kitts'
capital of Basseterre.) This is no place for your fancy togs. In fact,
the less you bring in the way of luggage, the happier you will be
when you try to get here.

*THE COCKLESHELL, Box 284, St. Kitts, West Indies. There is no
telephone, but if you get on the island and want to reach the
Bowers, go to Ocean Terrace Inn and ask them how to do it.
When the Cockleshell boat comes to town, the boatman always
checks at OTI. The 10 rooms all have a sea view; the newer units
have a balcony.*

*Getting there: Fly to St. Kitts from San Juan, Puerto Rico, or from
Sint Maarten, or from St. Croix, United States Virgin Islands. Take
a taxi from the airport to the dock at Basseterre if the Bowers are
expecting you. If they are not, go to OTI and check as to the
whereabouts of the boatman. Once in the boat, count on a 45-
minute, sometimes wet and splashy ride.*

**RAWLINS PLANTATION, on a highspot of the 260-acre estate,
inland from the fishing village of Dieppe Bay, on the northern
curve of the island of St. Kitts.**

When you pull into the parking area just below the porch of
the main house, you will feel as though you have arrived at
someone's private home. You have, in fact.

The Walwyns opened their plantation for a handful of visitors in 1973, and have continued their pattern of paying houseguests since that time. When I arrived here for the first time, it was late afternoon and I had driven up the east coast, past historic Brimstone Hill, the stone fort that has perched on its clifftop since it was built by the English and then the French in the 18th century. The half-dozen people who were spending their holidays at Rawlins Plantation had gathered on the terrace for some conversation with the Walwyns and their son Philip, who was getting ready to enter his huge catamaran in the single-handed trans-Atlantic race.

The view from the porch, and elsewhere on the well-kept grounds, is a Caribbean classic, with islands punctuating the blue Caribbean and long sweeps of green, mostly sugar cane in season, stretching to the blue sea.

An informal, British-style atmosphere prevails. Meals are usually served in the main building, which was built in 1970 on the foundation of the old sugar factory, but you can have lunch at the side of the small pool if you don't want to leave the sun.

There are some beaches a short drive away and the plantation car will take you there, although northcoast Kittitian beaches are not some of the Caribbean's best. They are usually grey pebbly sand.

Excursions can include sailing or flying to nearby islands; going to the rugged Black Rocks on the surf-pounded east coast for a picnic; into Basseterre, a half hour drive down either coast, for a day in the West Indian town; or an afternoon at Brimstone Hill Fortress, lingering long enough to watch the sunset from there. Among the off-island options are the opportunities to go for a sail with Philip on his catamaran, for a fishing excursion which the Walwyns will assist in arranging, or on a number of longer excursions such as taking the daily ferry to Nevis or flying by small plane to other nearby islands such as Statia, Saba, or even St. Maarten.

You'll need a car for traveling around the island, and plenty of books, paints, or sharpened pencils, and a writing tablet to occupy the leisure hours at the plantation. The Walwyns are true to their stated goal of "offering personal attention and absolute tranquility."

RAWLINS PLANTATION, Mount Pleasant, P.O. Box 340, St. Kitts, West Indies. Telephone: St. Kitts 6-221. The 6 rooms of the inn are in cottages, each with its own modern bathroom, hot and cold running water, and comfortable furnishings. One of the most unusual rooms is in the 250-year-old windmill tower, where guests enjoy a sitting room and an upstairs bedroom with an antique four-poster bed. Some cottages have efficiency units.

Getting there: You can fly to St. Kitts from the bigger and better serviced airports of Puerto Rico, St. Thomas, St. Croix, or St. Maarten. Ask for Dash when you clear customs at the St. Kitts Airport or, if he is busy, negotiate with one of the other drivers to take you to the north (a half hour drive). The fare is about $30 E.C.

FAIRVIEW INN, north of the airport, about five minutes inland from Boyd's Village.

Arriving at the Fairview Inn is like coming to your summer home. The main building is a home and has been for generations of Kittitians. Once part of a plantation, the wood frame house has all the trimmings you'll learn to expect from West Indian Great Houses—the verandah, louvered windows, and main rooms open to the tropical breezes. The house dates from the 18th century, when the building was a French plantation owner's home.

Present owners, Freddy and Betty Lam, have added their personal touches and remodeled following their own designs, almost 10 years ago. Taking the cue from Betty Lam's Kittitian family, Trinidad-born Freddy put his expertise to work to make the inn a popular spot for off-island overnight visitors and island residents who come for meals.

Tropical flowers cascade over the grounds, planted and pruned under the watchful eye of Betty Lam. There's a huge bougainvillea "tree" at the back of the house that blooms in a spectacular range of reds, from corals to magenta. You'll pass it on the way from the dining room to your cottage.

A small swimming pool makes the inland location acceptable to those of us who must have water within a few paces when we are in the Caribbean. More than once during my island travels, I have set up my typewriter in a corner of the terrace where the bougainvillea tumbles over the walls and fences and where I can take a refreshing glance at the pool and the hills behind.

Justifiably known for her recipes, Betty Lam incorporates local produce into delicious menus—offering you callaloo (soup), breadfruit, local fish and other West Indian favorites. If you like West Indian flavoring, try her homemade hot sauce that is HOT. For dessert, hope that they'll have the mango pie on the menu when you visit. My mouth waters at the thought.

Some of the staff have been with the Lams since the start and the few who are new are Kittitians from the neighborhood or perhaps their friends or relatives from nearby sister-island Nevis. They are the best sources for things to do on the island and, if possible on their day off, may lead you personally to their home villages and favorite island places.

FAIRVIEW INN, Box 212, Basseterre, St. Kitts, West Indies. Telephone: 2472. A few of the bedrooms are in the main building, but most of the 30 rooms are in cottages that have been built up the hill behind the main house, where the plantation outbuildings used to stand. All rooms are modern, simply (but adequately) furnished, with private bath, telephone, and other modern comforts. Most are two per cottage, each with its own small porch.

Getting there: Fly to St. Kitts from Puerto Rico on Prinair via St. Thomas or St. Croix and Sint Maarten, or fly via LIAT from Antigua. The inn is a 15-minute taxi ride up the coast, from the airport.

GOLDEN LEMON, Dieppe Bay, St. Kitts, W.I.

"In 1962 when I was looking for a place in the islands, all islands looked alike," Arthur Leaman told me a few years ago. The American Virgins were too expensive and, although he was attracted by St. Lucia, it rained for a solid week while he was there. So he headed north to St. Kitts where he found a ramshackle house at Dieppe Bay. Part of the house had been built by the French in 1625. The English added the upstairs in a "sort of Georgian" style. Termites had been the only permanent guests for too many years.

One of the first investments Leaman made in his dream house was about $5000 to wrap the house in a bag and fumigate it to try to get rid of the termites. And that was after a close friend had advised him not "to buy too much to do." For most of the time the project has been under way, Arthur Leaman has shuttled between jobs in New York and his island haven. On most of his return trips he has been accompanied by things like generators, voltage regulators, and other items necessary to keep the place running, as well as a selection of Third Avenue antiques to supplement the island furniture he has been able to pick up around St. Kitts.

The Golden Lemon is now an oasis—with a small pool in the entry courtyard, a grey sand beach shared with local fishermen, and a grove of coconut palms just outside its gates. Inside, the rooms are picture perfect: overhead fans and louvered windows and doors (no air-conditioning), four-poster beds, island antiques for the most part, and flowers in the rooms—and all around. Leaman estimates he has put about three times the purchase price into the decorating, and the place looks like it.

Tucked into the fishing village of Dieppe Bay, at the north end of St. Kitts, the hotel is haven for many of the village residents. For several years, a Kittitian woman faithfully stitched for hotel guests, either from patterns they brought with them, or from ideas of her own, worked on fabric that could be bought in Basseterre, about 13 miles down the coast and the island's capital. The job can still be done for interested guests. Another local woman brews sorrel for New Year's eve, buying the berries in the market, drying them in the sun and brewing them into that pungent drink well-known to islanders. And the kitchen staff, steeped in the spices and fresh fish tradition of the West Indies, serves island foods in typical sauces, for piquant meals that guests try to recreate when they get home.

Golden Lemon is a quiet place on a quiet island. (Leaman

says it "takes a week and a half to get used to slowing down.") There's not a lot of action, no tennis, organized water sports, or planned activities, although there is golf at Frigate Bay about 20 miles down the coast. There's plenty of time to do what you want.

GOLDEN LEMON, Dieppe Bay, St. Kitts, W.I. Telephone: St. Kitts 7-260. The 7 rooms are all personalized. No two are alike. There's a melange of antique furnishings and plenty of fresh air and tropical flowers outside the windows. On the shore. Small but pretty pool.

Getting there: St. Kitts is reached via small plane flight on Prinair from Puerto Rico, with stops at St. Croix or St. Thomas, and St. Maarten, or via LIAT from Antigua. Taxis make the 13-mile trip up the coast from the airport.

OCEAN TERRACE INN, Basseterre, overlooking the town, St. Kitts, W.I.

Unassuming to look at from the front gate, the inn holds a wealth of West Indian hospitality within. The main building is relatively new, with little historic value, but the rooms are pleasant and the food served in the dining room is among the island's best.

The swimming pool gives the inn an added asset, especially if you have to be in town for business. Ocean Terrace Inn is convenient, a short taxi ride from the center, and a popular place for local business lunches.

Not quite a traditional inn, Ocean Terrace Inn is included because of its in-town situation and the fact that Colin Pereira is a good host. Among the activities he arranges for guests are walks or hikes into the rain forest (he serves as guide), and day trips along the Kittitian coast or to the nearby islands of Nevis or Statia, aboard his 25-foot fibre glass cruiser (which is also available for week-long diving holidays).

Some lodging rooms are in the main building, which also houses the discotheque on the bottom floor, just off the swimming pool. The season of 1977-78 saw the addition of 12 new rooms in a modern building just down the slope from street level.

OCEAN TERRACE INN, Box 65, Fortlands, St. Kitts, West Indies. Telephone: 2754 or 2380. The 17 rooms in the main building come in a variety of shapes and sizes, room 33 being a small single at a low rate with no air conditioning. Twelve newer air-conditioned rooms are in the building down the hill, just below the swimming pool. All have completely modern furnishings, not fancy, but certainly comfortable. The main dining room is popular with Kittitians, as are the lounge areas and poolside facilities.

Getting there: From the airport, the ride to OTI takes about 5 minutes. Charge is usually $2 E.C.

MONTPELIER ESTATE, on a hill with a beautiful view of the rolling Nevisian hills and the high peaks.

There is a lot of history connected to the Montpelier Estate, but I have never been able to get the stories straight. Perhaps you'll have better luck if you stay here long enough to talk at length to Spencer Byron and his wife who are the local managers. As best I understand it, the Estate belonged to a Nisbet relative—some have told me that it was the father-in-law of Admiral Horatio Nelson who, as you may know, married Fanny Nisbet at the Fig Tree Church not far from here. Nelson was stationed at English Harbour, Antigua, at the time.

The specific details of the history never matter for long, once I get to this spot, look at the view, and settle into the very comfortable main house which has been constructed in the old coral stone and cement style. The old mill still stands, and the sugar building has been roofed over as the bar and lounge area.

When I ate here, the dinner was excellent Nevisian fare, served by candlelight, which added to the glamor of a breeze-swept, star-filled evening.

There is a mammoth pool which I found to be seldom used, and a tennis court in the blazing sun that was not inviting to me, but may be to you. Perhaps it would be playable early in the morning or at sundown. Suggestive of the salubrious atmosphere here was the five-year-old *Clipper Magazine* that was in a prime spot on a table in the lounge.

MONTPELIER ESTATE, St. John's Parish, Box 20, Nevis, West Indies. Telephone: 462. The 19 rooms are scattered around the property in a variety of buildings and with a variety of views. Furnishings are simple, but attractive, with colorful accents. Most of the out-buildings in which the rooms are located are built in traditional style so that the Estate still looks like a plantation.

Getting there: Fly to Nevis from Antigua or St. Croix on a small plane. You may have to charter to get here when you want to, but check with the management about the best way to reach Nevis when you plan to come. From the airport, count on a $10 U.S. ride for about half an hour, and for your sake, I hope that the road has been repaired since I last bounced and jounced over it.

NISBET PLANTATION, not far from the airport on Nevis, W.I.

This plantation has everything, including a lovely half-mile of beach and a house full of legends. A working plantation for most of its life, Nisbet opened for guests under the aegis of Mary Pomeroy, something of an island legend herself. An intrepid woman with a temper far larger than her size, Mary had some run-ins with the local government and left the island in her small plane, piloted by herself, several years ago.

Her plantation-turned-inn was managed by others for awhile and finally, in the early 1970s, was taken in tow by Geoffrey Boon, a seventh generation Kittitian and a London-educated lawyer. He now runs a fine inn.

The plantation atmosphere prevails, with guests who settle down to enjoy a game of darts and lively conversation at the main house, or who choose horseback riding, swimming, hiking, biking, or swinging in a hammock during days of leisure. Meals are served family style, with guests encouraged to mix and mingle.

Set amid 30 acres of coconut plantation with tall palms standing like sentinels, Nisbet's legends date to the days when young Fanny Nisbet, eventual wife of Horatio Nelson and an island heroine, came here to play at her relatives' house.

The simple (original) accommodations in the main house are being phased out for guests, so prime spots in my opinion are the two older buildings: Cox Heath (named for Victor Cox who wintered here until well into his 80's) and Gingerlands (named for one of the island villages, as are all the cottages). Others might prefer the newer buildings, including those added for the 1977-78 season, all of which are folded discreetly into the landscape.

NISBET PLANTATION, Nevis, W.I. Telephone: 325. All 20 rooms are in outbuildings, most of them octagonal cottages scattered around the property. Rooms are modern, clean and neat, with overhead fans and louvered windows, plus a small porch for leisurely sitting.

Getting there: Nisbet is less than 5 minutes by taxi from the airport. When the mood is right, Geoff Boon may meet you himself in Antiqua or St. Kitts in his own small plane. Otherwise you can take commercial flights on LIAT or come by boat across the Nevis channel from St. Kitts.

CRONEY'S OLD MANOR ESTATE, not far from the village of Gingerland, Nevis, W.I.

Originally a sugar plantation, in 1806 the estate was turned into a stud farm for breeding slaves, according to one legend. In 1834, when slavery was abolished, the property returned again to sugar and to Sea Island cotton. It's come a long way since then.

A true estate swept into shape as a modern inn by a group of Texas investors, the name Croney comes from a former owner who was promised this kind of immortality if he sold the property.

Most of the old stone and mortar buildings have been refurbished and refitted with new interiors that maintain the plantation atmosphere. No detail has been spared to make the place comfortable, with its huge rooms furnished with antiques—or good reproductions. The original Great House was built in 1832. It had marble floors, high ceilings, and intricate wood work made by European craftsmen. All has been restored, and in addition there is a swimming pool, surrounded by

several gathering spots. There's a small shop on the premises, but the handful of stores in Gingerland are worth seeing, too. (Don't expect to buy lavish gifts. Life is simple here in spite of appearance.)

Depending on the management and your fellow guests, this out-of-the-way inn can be homelike. Even without the palatial house, the surroundings are enough by themselves to put you into a soporific West Indian plantation mood, providing peace and quiet is what you are seeking.

Planned originally as a condominium project, the home-purchase plan seems to be slow getting underway. In the meantime, the rest of us can enjoy this unusual inn.

The plantation itself is still operating and provides most of the food at the table.

CRONEY'S OLD MANOR ESTATE, Box 70, Gingerland, Nevis, W.I. Telephone: 445. Guests in the 10 units have a variety of accommodations, some of them spacious duplexes. All are large, modern and expensively furnished. Comfort and appearance have been given every attention. Children are welcome, especially in the two-bedroom suites. For details, the Dallas office can be reached c/o NEVCO LTD., 126 Meadows Building, Dallas, Texas 75206. Telephone (214) 369-5136.

Getting there: Take a taxi from the Nevis Airport on the rim road around the island, either through Charlestown or around the other way. Allow about 45 minutes to reach the estate.

GOLDEN ROCK, on a hill, about an hour's drive around the rim of the island from the airport, passing through Charlestown.

Pam and Frank Barry first came to Nevis to settle into the island life, making goatskin pocket books and eventually working with some of the Nevisians to teach them how to cure and pattern the skins. It was a sort of Peace Corps project, but it led to the Barry's interest in taking over the management of what had been Pam's great-great-grandfather's estate. Legends are rife as you talk to the Barrys and others who know the history of this particular plantation. There's a garden where the old Great House once stood, and there are ruins all around. They punctuate some of the history.

The Galeys are the people who opened this former estate, or what was left of it, as an inn in 1957. They bought about 200 acres of the property, and still own some of it, in a consortium with others. The Sugar Mill that dates from 1815 forms part of the inn, and cottages with two double rooms, each with its own porch area, make up the lodging rooms.

The tennis court that is behind the main gathering spot is used by guests, and the dart board is one of the favorite sunset pastimes. The inn is not a luxury place, but it is ideal for people who have made the long and multi-change trip to get to a place where peace, quiet, and congenial guests are assured.

Those who love the beach have a choice of several coves, all a short drive down the hill and around the shoreline.

GOLDEN ROCK, St. George Parish, Nevis, West Indies. Telephone: 346. The 10 rooms are nothing spectacular and, when I visited most recently, showed signs of wear and the effects of sun and sea breezes, but somehow that doesn't matter when you settle in to enjoy the hospitality.

Getting there: The airstrip on Nevis is best reached by small plane from nearby Antigua which has direct flights from major cities. It's also possible to fly to Nevis from St. Croix, in the United States Virgin Islands, where a charter service has been operating flights for Nevisian visitors. (When you inquire about reservations, ask the Barrys about the best way to get to Nevis when you plan to go. Things change.)

ST. LUCIA

If you're lured by an island that counts 132 beaches and is speckled with ruins of forts from the 17th and 18th century days when allegiance was tossed from English to French with the rapidity of a ball crossing the net at a tennis match, then St. Lucia's your spot. One of a handful of Associated States of England, most of them granted that status in the late 1960s, St. Lucia prepares for independence with some of the Caribbean's most complete vacation facilities—and a local building rule that outlaws any building higher than a royal palm.

An oval-shaped island just south of French Martinique, St. Lucia's local patois shows the influence of France—as do the cooking, the costumes worn at festivals and some of the festivals themselves. The lush terrain and a spine of mountains that run the length of the island, are effectively pinpointed by the two most spectacular peaks in the Caribbean. St. Lucia's Pitons rise from the southwestern shore and have been landmarks for sailors since the time of Columbus, and perhaps before that.

Arriving on St. Lucia can be confusing until you realize that there are two airports. Hewanorra is the airport at the south, served by the big jets from the United States, Europe, Canada, and elsewhere in the Caribbean. Vigie Airport, the island's first airstrip, is about a five-minute drive from the capital of Castries, midway in the island's west coast and about an hour's wiggly drive north of Hewanorra. Ships come into Castries harbor on cruises out of San Juan as well as on some of the longer cruises from Florida, and yachts anchor at protected harbors at Rodney Bay, Marigot Bay, and Castries itself.

Star attractions are the St. Lucians, some of the Caribbean's most hospitable folk. You'll meet them in Castries at market day, and around the island as you tour by taxi or rental car. The Pitons are best viewed from the sea, but you can drive near them on the way to Soufrière, the village named for the drive-in volcano in the hills behind it.

Action options focus on the water, with sailing leading the list. A cruise along the west coast with a picnic lunch should fill one day. You can tour plantations, visit the volcano's sulphurous jets (where your taxi-guide will cook an egg in the steam), go horseback riding, or shop in Castries. There's a golf course at La Toc Hotel, south of Castries, and another near Cariblue Hotel at the northern quarter of the island. Some hotels have tennis courts. Don't count on any big-time nightlife; most of the action will be at the hotels.

Best beaches are speckled with hotels and, since the beaches are not long, most will be decorated with hotel guests. West coast coves have the most placid sea; surf pounds on the east coast and swimming there should only be in the hands of a native. The longest stretch of sand is the five miles that stretches in front of the Halcyon Days Hotel, not far from Hewanorra Airport at the southern tip, near the town of Vieux Fort.

For further information, the St. Lucia Tourist Board has an office at 220 East 42nd Street, New York, New York 10017. Telephone: (212) 867-2950. On St. Lucia, the Tourist Board office is near the marketplace at the harbor at Castries, St. Lucia, West Indies. (25¢ postage per half-ounce airmail.)

ANSE CHASTANET, Soufrière, St. Lucia, W.I.

My first glimpse of Anse Chastanet (Chastanet Beach) was of a curve of silver sand, seen from the water. I had sailed in with friends, boarding their yacht at Castries harbor and cruising south along the west coast of St. Lucia. We dropped anchor, dove off and swam to shore, stepping ashore on one of the island's small sandy coves. It looked as though it belonged only to the fishermen at work on their nets at the end of the beach.

Not so. Up in the lush green hills that rise from the water are a handful of octagonal cottages, a small main house with a couple of single rooms and one and two-bedroom suites as well as two villas that would be easy to call home.

A weekend haven for St. Lucians from the capital city of Castries, the small inn also has a following of independent travelers who prefer their tropical retreats pure. Max and Joana Dahinden manage the inn. One of the owners, Nick Troobitscoff, an architect, has spruced up the place since my first visit, but has, thankfully, managed to maintain the West Indian Eden aura.

One improvement is a beachside bar and restaurant area decorated with St. Lucian fishermen's boats that double as buffet tables. The food is local and excellent. It is prepared and served at the beach and at the house up the hill by the St. Lucians who live in nearby villages.

The original property was built between 1967 and 1969 by the Cummings family and was operated by them until its purchase in 1975 by Nick Troobitscoff and Wayne Brown.

The climb from the beach can be a tough one. There are 102 steps, but the management has thoughtfully provided bird cages at appropriate intervals and nature has arranged a spectacular view, so its perfectly natural, if not downright necessary, to pause and look along the way.

Activities are best suited to those who love the outdoors. The Pitons, St. Lucia's two spectacular peaks (one rising to 2,619 feet and the other to a mere 2,461 feet), can be seen from most rooms. There's a botanical garden not far outside the grounds, with signs marking every tree. Included are Midshipman's Butter, Salt Fish Wood, and hundreds of other West Indian plants, identified by their local names. For those who want to walk the half hour to Anse Mamin, there's the opportunity to talk with Mr. Albert Senac, the overseer, who will take you around and tell you about the plants and the histories of the old plantation houses.

The town of Soufrière is the old West Indies at its best, with a church its focal point and a lively marketplace. A couple of good restaurants (Ruins and The Still) are fine for diversion, and you'll

155

find enough to keep you interested for weeks—if this is your kind of place.

ANSE CHASTANET, Box 216, Soufrière, St. Lucia, West Indies. Telephone: 7355. There are 38 rooms, some in the main house, others as one-bedroom suites or two suites with two bedrooms, all with kitchenettes, plus 14 cottages and two villas, each with four bedrooms and four bathrooms, making them ideal for large families. All rooms have overhead fans and a view of either the Pitons or the Caribbean, both glorious. Complete refurbishing during the summer of 1976 and close attention since keeps everything looking good.

Getting there: St. Lucia has two airports. Big jets fly into the southern one, Hewanorra, and from there it is about an hour's wiggly drive to Anse Chastanet. I suggest a driver since none of the roads are posted and, although it is not really difficult, it might be hard to find the first time around. The other arrival routes are by sea from Castries (my preference), or driving south from the Vigie Airport at Castries along the snaky, up and down, poorly paved west coast road. A pretty trip, but exhausting, taking two to three hours for a novice. Getting there is not "half the fun." Being there is.

DASHEENE, at eye level with the Pitons, St. Lucia's twin peaks that are more spectacular than any of their many pictures.

When you've bumped and rolled along the road to get here from St. Lucia's southern airport at Vieux Fort, you may wonder (as I often do) what prompted anyone to build a place like this "way out here." Just walk through the doors of the first villa, and you'll understand. The view is one of the Caribbean's most spectacular. The lush green coat that reaches the points of the Pitons slides all the way down to the seacoast below; the bottom half of the green coat is a banana plantation.

The air at this perch is an elixir. Any cares you may have brought with you vanish as soon as you settle into one of the units, where you will be setting up housekeeping for the length of your stay. Management provides maid service to take the pain out of the chore.

Dasheene appeals primarily to self-sufficient types, those who do not need a lot of planned entertainment and who are happy to have a quiet, sometimes solitary holiday. While manager John Gates and the rest of the staff do their utmost to see that all your wishes are cheerfully realized, there are the vagaries of getting to and from this spot, of finding out which of the small restaurants in the town of Soufrière is serving what, when, and—if you haven't rented a car—of trying to negotiate the time to go to and to be picked up from the beach at Anse Chastanet, a 20-minute ride around the coast on the other side of Soufrière. Guests at Dasheene are welcome to use the beach at the neighboring small inn, since there is only the spring-fed pool for dunking at this lofty level.

Meals are sometimes served at the main unit, if the guests would like to have a special meal and the house-count warrants. You can check when you arrive.

DASHEENE, Milaclaire Ltd., Box 225, Soufrière, St. Lucia, West Indies. Telephone: Soufrière 7444. The eight units are cheek-by-jowl, in a line so that all share the view of the Pitons and sea. The 3-bedroom villas easily accommodate 6 people, with the living level complete with a comfortable inside lounging room, an open-air terrace, and a kitchen which opens into the dining area. Upstairs bedrooms are on either two or three levels with an open stairway linking the levels at interesting angles. Furnishings depend on the unit's owner, but will be homey, personalized, and comfortable. (If you fall in love with the place, as many have, you too can become a unit owner. John Gates will happily discuss the plans.)

Getting there: When your big jet lands at St. Lucia's southern tip Hewanorra International Airport, you will have a hefty 1½-hour ride ahead of you. If you have advised the management about your flight and expected arrival time, they will arrange for someone to meet you. If you arrive unannounced, you can hire one of the taxi drivers you'll find waiting eagerly. In either case, you'll pay about $20 U.S. for the ride to Dasheene.

EAST WINDS INN, at La Brelotte Bay on the west coast, north of Castries, St. Lucia, W.I.

On a recent visit at East Winds, I found owner Margaret Eggerer up to her elbows in piles of chicken and fixings for the evening meal. It was about 8 a.m. and she had been up for hours. Still her smile was friendly and she had ample time to visit.

That's the way this place is. The handful of cottages are tucked among trees, flowers, and bird cages, beachside at the

end of a side road off the main north-south west coast route. The pace is relaxed. Conversation in the haven of thatch, wood, and open air that serves as a gathering spot may run to favorite authors, or close friends who are creative. Bookshelves hold many popular titles, most of the books were read and left behind by guests.

The beach is white sand and, while not the longest on the island, is ideal for pre-breakfast or sunset swims and for all-day lounging. Visitors at other hotels and anyone else in-the-know are lured here on Sundays, especially for the mid-day buffet and day-long leisure with a house party air.

There are a few boats available (Sunfish and the like) for use by hotel guests, but all other activity will be what you find for yourself — renting a car for driving around the island or lounging in a hammock reading a book.

EAST WINDS INN, Box 193, Castries, St. Lucia, W.I. Telephone: 8212. The 10 units are all thatched "huts" with modern conveniences, built in rondavel style. Although there are simple cooking facitities in all units, many guests prefer to go to the beach bar for meals and conversation. The room furnishings may leave something to be desired if you prefer fancy furniture, but there's nothing lacking with the hospitality.

Getting there: Your plane will land at the south end Hewanorra Airport if you are coming from one of the big islands, or from the States. You can then take a two-hour taxi ride up the coast to Castries and beyond, or hop on the small plane for the flight to Castries Airport. From the Castries Airport the taxi takes about 15 minutes.

ST. VINCENT and its GRENADINE ISLANDS

Little known and long overlooked by brigades of tourists, St. Vincent and the several small Grenadine Islands that stretch south toward Grenada offer visitors the life that Robinson Crusoe found. Tied to England since that country's decisive defeat of the French in the 19th century, the Associated State is planning for independence.

The south coast of St. Vincent is the seat of the local government;Kingstown is the name of the main town and capital. But it is the several small specks that curve toward the south that offer the best hideaway spots in the Caribbean. By name, St. Vincent's Grenadines are Bequia, Petit Nevis, Battowia, Baliceaux, Isle Quartre, Mustique, Petit Mustique, Canouan, Mayreau, the Tobago Cays, Union Island, Palm Island, Petit St. Vincent and Petit Martinique.

Along the west coast of St. Vincent (the calmer shore), and from the island of Bequia, local fisherman set out to capture whales as they migrate south. At the north of St. Vincent, the island's volcano stands as temptation for climbers who make a day of the hike up one side and down the other.

Arriving on St. Vincent takes patience. Once you've gotten to Barbados, double check your reservations for the flight to St. Vincent. (If it has been cancelled, or you want to be sure of close connections, charter for the 45-minute flight.) Petit St. Vincent, Bequia and many of the other Grenadines are reached only by boat, either the mail boat service or by chartered yacht. There are air strips on Union Island and Mustique for small plane service.

Star attractions for St. Vincent are its volcano in the north, the marketplace at the east end of Kingstown, and the activity along the waterfront when the banana boats are loading. St. Vincent is a rural island with daily routines established by (and for) the residents. In the Grenadines, you'll find that life is tied to the sea. White sand beaches slope to the shore.

Action options involve the sea (for fishing, sailing, swimming, and some scuba), or a round of golf at the Aquaduct Golf Course, about a 20-minute drive from Kingstown. There's an island-operated casino at the golf course, near the clubhouse. Tennis can be played at Aquaduct, or at the court over the brow of the hill on Young Island, about 200 yards off the south shore of St. Vincent.

Nightlife is limited to island-oriented entertainment, perhaps a small band, a game of darts or conversation with Vincentians and the other hotel guests. There's not much more than that.

Best beaches are at the south coast of St. Vincent where there are some beige sandy coves. Most of the beaches elsewhere around St. Vincent are black-to-silver volcanic sand. Pure white powder rims most of the Grenadines, with the Tobago Cays a highlight for those who sail in to anchor for snorkeling, swimming, or a picnic. Bequia has white sand beaches at its coves.

For further information in the United States, contact the Caribbean Tourism Association, 20 East 46th Street, New York, New York 10017. Telephone: (212) 682-0435. The local office for the St. Vincent and Grenadine Islands Tourists Board is at Box 834, Kingstown, St. Vincent, West Indies. (25¢ postage per half-ounce airmail.)

HERON HOTEL, just across from the boat loading docks in the center of Kingstown.

There are only a handful of places like the Heron left in the Caribbean as I see it today. About 20 years ago, when I first visited St. Vincent, the Heron Hotel was one of the few places to stay.

I stayed on the second floor and entered through a nondescript doorway with a time-worn sign announcing it.

Most of the rooms had overhead fans, some had essential mosquito netting which you pulled around the bed at night, and few had a private bath. Walls were thin, hospitality was warm and your choice of lounging spots included a rocker in the center room, or a seat on the balcony where you could watch the activity below as the banana boats loaded.

Things haven't changed much since my first visit. More rooms have private baths, all have been painted and there are now modern mosquito repellents in most rooms—to do away with the mosquitos that still can come through the louvered windows.

This is a simple, traditional West Indian inn, well known to those nomads of the Caribbean who pass through St. Vincent regularly on business. The hotel still offers one of the best values in the islands, with a room rate that hovers at $15 per night, and

Mrs. Mackensie maintains the hospitality for which the place is known.

One addition in recent seasons was a dive shop on street level. Daniel Madura opened his Caribe Diving Center to provide scuba, snorkel, and expected dive facilities for those who have plunged to the Caribbean's depths elsewhere and want to be guided to good spots off the shores of St. Vincent. But that is about as modern as the Heron has gotten.

A few steps from the front door, the main street of Kingstown stretches along the waterfront. There are a few shops for visitors (Batik Caribe is noteworthy), but most of the commerce of this small West Indian town is strictly for the residents. If you have any interest in West Indian history, its worthwhile stopping at the Carnegie Library, a few streets inland from the banana boat docks.

HERON HOTEL, Box 226, Kingstown, St. Vincent, West Indies. Telephone: 71631. The 15 rooms vary in shape and size, but all are on the second floor, where the main dining room and reception desk are located. Some rooms have overhead fans, some are air-conditioned and most, now, have private bath. Accommodations are simple, adequate and very old-time West Indian.

Getting there: When you arrive at St. Vincent's airport (from Barbados, St. Lucia, or elsewhere), take a taxi into Kingstown. It's about a 10-minute ride.

MARINERS' INN, on the south shore of St. Vincent, with a clear view of Young Island and yachts at anchor.

The inn was the dream of Bill and Sandra Miller who fled the commercialism of Christiansted on St. Croix in the 1960s, when St. Croix threatened to become "overdeveloped." Bill had pioneered the watersports activities on St. Croix in the late 1950s, and did the same for those with a water interest when he built and opened his inn here on St. Vincent.

The flip-flops in managers/owners that you will know to be typical of the Caribbean if you've come down this way before has affected the history of Mariners' Inn. The Corrigans came from Vigie Beach in St. Lucia to run the place for awhile and, when I last looked, Lloyd and Laurie Gilles whom I first met at another Vincentian spot and then saw during their stint at managing

Croney's Old Manor on Nevis were here running Mariners' Inn.

The place had been pulled back into shape, at least into as much "shape" as anyone wants. Most people come here for rest and reviving, while swapping stories with sailors and other nautical types. The shoreside bar is a popular spot for droppers-in at all times of the day and night; the steel band entertainment evenings are popular with local folk as well as with guests who stay here and at the handful of other hotels. Standard entertainment that you can count on is conversation and a game of darts. Clothes are always casual and feet are often bare.

Mariners' Inn is a very casual place, and I'm sure no manager/owner will plan to change that aspect of the inn.

MARINERS' INN, Box 868, St. Vincent, West Indies. Telephone: 84287. The bedrooms are upstairs, over the dining room and the public area. Most of the eight rooms have heavy mahogany beds from St. Lucia; Room 17 has a sea view and a small balcony.

Getting there: St. Vincent is best reached via Barbados. There is regular plane service, but the printed schedule you may have in your hand doesn't mean anything. Check when you arrive in Barbados, and be prepared for delays. Once on St. Vincent, take a taxi for the 10-minute ride to Mariners' Inn. (From that point on, you can use the public bus service which passes along the road into Kingstown.)

YOUNG ISLAND, 200 yards off the south shore of St. Vincent, linked by frequent boat service.

John Houser had the vision to create a resort on this speck of an island, but when he first urged me to come to see what he had built, I planned my visit reluctantly. I like my islands pure, unencumbered with modern trappings, and John's history as a high-powered executive with Hilton International (one of the men who sparked the first moves by Hilton internationally, in fact) and then with American Express made me wary of what I would find here. He had assured me that he had assembled the best of all the resorts he had found while traveling around the world. I envisioned a lively, super-sophisticated highrise, the kind of building that was popular with developers in the Caribbean in the early 1960s—and popular with Hilton and American Express group travel.

I was wrong, and delighted. I found an island "paradise" which has been a perfect retreat for me on many occasions when writing deadlines close in and I need a quiet place to hide. On several occasions, that place has been cottage 17, a south-sea-island-style haven with a spectacular view of mountains and Caribbean Sea. Basic comforts are here, with subtle and thoughtful extras, but the overall theme is nature—and that may mean that the water system fails or that the lights go out, both of which are common small Caribbean island problems. There's a Robinson Crusoe atmosphere here, with touches of elegance aided by a caring staff.

Young Island, John and Polly Houser's dream, is a speck in the sea just off the south shore of St. Vincent. Yachts anchor in the span of sea between Young Island's small beach and the Vincentian shore, nestling into the protected harbor and adding

an air of adventure to the activity at the small inn. Many of the yachtsmen anchoring here have made the Grenadines their first landfall after a Trans-Atlantic crossing.

As with many dreams, the Housers found a gap between their vision and the reality. The project proved to involve an endless warren of hard-to-impossible confrontations. Getting permits from the local government at a time when they knew nothing about the resort business was only one of the problems. Bringing in fresh water, electricity, building materials and then foodstuffs proved to be a constant challenge. Hiring and training Vincentians, most of whom had never seen a hotel before, had never worked in one and certainly had never stayed in one, required endless patience, tolerance, and understanding. After a decade of owning and managing, the Housers retired from the project and moved north, leaving the property to the new owner, Charles MacCulloch from Nova Scotia.

Some things have changed with the times. A tennis court was added, up and over the hill that rises in the middle of the 20-acre island. A resort-owned yacht, *Patricia of Camelot*, sits at anchor except when it is taking guests on a cruise through the string of Grenadines. There is entertainment on some evenings in winter.

But the basic atmosphere established by the Housers—the 24 individual cottages nestled in their own bowered surroundings, with private terrace, and an outdoor shower discretely fenced for modest types; the Tahitian-style central building that is the gathering spot; the staff who have been with the place since it opened; and the sunsets over the hills of St. Vincent across the water—hasn't changed at all. I still love the place, and am happy to be welcomed by Vidal Browne, one of John Houser's first Vincentian employees who is now general manager of the inn.

YOUNG ISLAND, St. Vincent, West Indies. Telephone: St. Vincent 84826. The 24 villas that are hidden in the foliage around the 20-acre island are one-room affairs, set up as a lounge area during daytime hours. Dressing room and toilet are in a separate room with open-air, bamboo-screened outside shower. Most villas have a terrace; some villas border the shore. Number 17, up the hill, is the highest climb, but it also has one of the best views, and a large terrace.

Getting there: Advise arrival time in advance, so that a taxi driver is waiting at the airport with your name in hand. Fly first to Barbados, for connection to St. Vincent (and be prepared for delayed flights from Barbados, where you may have to spend the night). LIAT flies between Barbados and St. Vincent in about 45 minutes. From the airport, it's about a 10-minute taxi ride to the Young Island pier where the boatman will be waiting (or will come across the channel when he sees you on the pier).

FRIENDSHIP BAY HOTEL, on Friendship Bay, "across" the island of Bequia from better known and busier Admiralty Bay.

Have you been to a Maine woods camp? Move it mentally to a remote and verdant tropical island, and you can picture Friendship Bay Hotel. This is a personality place—and the main personality is that of the creator and owner, Captain Niels Peter Thomsen, who retired from the U.S. Coast Guard more than 20 years ago and loves to talk about those years as though they were yesterday. For several years after his retirement Captain Thomsen owned and operated a mailboat, the *Expansion,* and he now keeps his aging 90-foot, two-masted Baltic trading schooner, *Lilli,* anchored offshore (as a prop for pictures if not also for a day sail around the islands).

Do not count on anything fancy here, in spite of the brochure's elaborate statements about the meats being "flown in from New York daily" and the "finest imported wines obtainable." You can be assured of the fact, that the fish is "caught in the bay" or elsewhere around Bequia and that "most of the vegetables come straight from the hotel's own gardens." Both of these facts alone should be enough to assure good to excellent meals.

Breakfast is served on the long verandah of the main house, and your room may be a simple "box" here also. (Alternatives are the rooms in a couple of other buildings on the grounds.)

This is a casual, outdoors kind of place where the sun and the sea offer not only the best daytime diversions, but also the source for most of the conversation that comes during and after the sunset.

FRIENDSHIP BAY HOTEL, Bequia, c/o St. Vincent, West Indies. Telephone: 83222. Each of the 28 double rooms have a private verandah porch and a view overlooking the sea. Each room has hot and cold running water, simple furnishings, and trade wind air-conditioning which makes mechanical air-conditioners unnecessary. Most of the rooms are in the rambling, wood main building; some are in separate cottages. All public rooms are in the main house which is on the hill overlooking the bay and beach.

Getting there: Fly to Barbados for the small plane connection, via charter or scheduled service, to St. Vincent. Take a taxi to Kingstown for the boat to Bequia and, on arrival at Admiralty Bay, take a Bequia taxi across the island to Friendship Bay and the hotel. Allow for delays at all transition points. You'll probably be happier about the entire excursion if you break it with an overnight, either in Barbados or in St. Vincent, depending on the boat schedule out of St. Vincent for Bequia. (If the boat leaves early, you'll have to stay overnight in St. Vincent; if you can get an afternoon boat, an overnight in Barbados still gives you time to get to St. Vincent).

SUNNY CARIBBEE, on the beach at 'Admiralty Bay, where the boats dock at the Grenadine Island of Bequia.

When Gerry and Jan Palmer built this place about a dozen years ago, their loyal following from the inn they had operated for many years on St. Vincent came along. The hospitality that they had made the key of their hillside perch on St. Vincent was recreated here at the shore of Admiralty Bay, and Jan's touches with fruit and flower arrangements, plus her marvelous decorating sense, made it seem as though the Sunny Caribbee had been part of the landscape for years.

When Rory Annesley and his wife bought the place in the mid-1970s, they pledged to continue the trademarks of the Palmers' touch, and have added a lot of their own special personalities as well. Guests can enjoy the fresh water swimming pool (although I've never been able to understand why anyone wants a pool when the entire Caribbean stretches out before you), a tennis court, and the use of the Annesleys' 34-foot yacht, "Oh Life," for day sailing around the Grenadines.

This is a casual place for sea-oriented folk. And, frankly, it is only those who love the sea who will ever make it to the island of Bequia. Once you've reached St. Vincent, which you can do via a big plane-small plane combination of flights, you have to go to the docks to be sure that the boat you've been told to take is still running. If it is, chances are it will be running late. (You should start relaxing when you arrive on St. Vincent. Nothing moves very fast from that point on.)

Passage across the Bequia Channel can be rough, whether you go aboard one of the sturdy island sloops or the motor mail and /or freight boats. Count the excursion as part of your holiday experience, and be sure to change from city clothes in the Barbados Airport if you haven't done so before that.

As for Sunny Caribbee, planned entertainment doesn't go much beyond the twice weekly informal barbecue and dance evenings, but there are several small spots (Frangipani is one of them) along the shore and in the village for some island conversation. The evening meal in the dining room of the main house always features island food, as well as some cosmopolitan treats.

Your daytime diversions can include fishing, snorkeling, and scuba diving at coves around Bequia, as well as an island excursion by jeep. I've always found that the first few days are filled with strolls into the village, naps in the sun, and dips in the sea. The beachside bar is open during the day for snacks and cooling potions.

SUNNY CARIBBEE, Bequia, c/o St. Vincent, West Indies. Telephone: St. Vincent 83244. The 17 cabanas string along the shore, with comfortable, camp-style rooms. All have verandahs and private bathrooms. Life is simple and beach oriented. There are 8 rooms in the main house, a colonial-style, wood-frame house in which the main dining room and the reading room are also located.

Getting there: Be sure to let the Annesleys know when you are coming and, if you make your plans far enough in advance, they will let you know "how" for the time you plan to cross from St. Vincent. The general route is to fly to Barbados, to charter a small plane or take the small plane "scheduled" service to St. Vincent, where you will take a taxi into the Kingstown docks to find out about boats for Bequia. If you want to take it slow, make overnight plans for Barbados or St. Vincent enroute.

FRANGIPANI, on the shore at Port Elizabeth, looking out on Bequia's Admiralty Bay.

This is one of my favorite inns, but no one who demands finger-snapping service should bother to make their way over to Bequia to find it. The personality of this place is the special personality of the family who have called Frangipani home for a long, long time. Sonny Mitchell was Premier of St. Vincent and its Grenadines at a young age; I think he was in his late 20s when voted to that office in the late 1960s. Even then, he could be found over here at his island home when the pressures of work allowed, and all during his term of office, which ended with the elections of 1974, his Canadian wife, Pat, and her colleague, Marie Kingston, ran this inn in a simple and special way.

Frangipani is first and foremost a home. The facilities are comfortable, in the best West Indian tradition. There's plenty of good seafood (fresh from the sea that splashes at your feet) and good island beverages, as well as fresh fruits and vegetables that grow on Bequia. At mealtimes and between, the porch at Frangipani is a favorite gathering spot for nautical types who come off their yachts anchored offshore, and for some of the exiles from more commercial areas who have chosen to make their home on Bequia where they can lead the simple life.

FRANGIPANI, Port Elizabeth, Bequia, c/o St. Vincent, West Indies. Telephone: 83255. The 6 rooms in the main house are my favorites. You have to walk a few doors down the hall for the bathroom. The wood walls are thin, so if you're a light sleeper, or make a lot of noise, perhaps you should request one of the 4 rooms in the building up the hill. That building was put up a couple of years ago "for those who like a bit of luxury." Each room has a private bathroom.

Getting there: Bequia assures that its visitors will be seaworthy by insisting that arrival be by boat. There's no other way to get here. You have a choice of motorboat service on somewhat of a schedule (which you should check when you arrive in St. Vincent, no matter what you've been advised when you made your hotel reservations), or sailboat. My preference is for arrival by sail, aboard an island-built schooner, but that can't always be arranged. To get this far, you will have flown to St. Vincent on a small plane from Barbados in about 45 minutes. Then take a 10-minute taxi ride to the docks at Kingstown, where you will be loaded aboard with freight and mail. The crossing takes about an hour.

PALM ISLAND BEACH CLUB, on Palm Island, one of the Grenadine Islands.

As happened with other adventurers in the 1960s, John and Mary Caldwell sailed by this island and decided they "had to have it." At that time, John Caldwell was operating in the Grenadines as a charter boat captain. His history with the sea is a long one. When he was 27, at the end of World War II, he sailed from Panama to Australia to pick up his Australian wife, Mary. His tale of adventures during the 106 days he covered 8500 miles in a small boat, with two kittens for company, is told in his book *Desperate Voyage*. He later sailed with his family in a 45-foot ketch, and recounted those adventures in his book *Family at Sea*. Today he maintains a small charter fleet of yachts for day and longer sails; all are moored offshore.

But the story that interests those of us in search of island

hideaways is the one that resulted in the change of this island's name from Prune Island, as this speck appears on many charts, to Palm Island. *That* process started with the tireless planting by John and Mary of what are now 8000 palm trees.

The palm trees punctuate most of the 110-acre island, all of which is available for roaming by guests at the small resort. Although many of the former guests have invested in property and now own their own homes on Palm Island (nee Prune Island), the hub of activity for most is the small hotel cluster of 20 stone-walled villas that opened in 1968.

Activity for guests is centered around the sea—either on it, in it, looking at it or talking about it. There is a tennis court, but you should also bring some good books to read. Otherwise the activity is as lively as the folks who sail in to anchor offshore.

There's a small shop for provisions if you are staying in one of the homes-available-for-rent-in-owner's-absence, but for more congenial and conversational surroundings, head for the beach house or the main building.

PALM ISLAND BEACH CLUB, Palm Island, ç/o St. Vincent, West Indies. Telephone: St. Vincent 88222. The 20 rooms vary depending upon whether you are in those used as the hotel cluster, all of which are scattered near the main building, or in one of the homes for rent. Overhead fans supplement tradewinds for your breeze, and the hot water may not flow as freely as you are used to having it at home. This is an outdoor-oriented Caribbean inn, with a casual, comfortable atmosphere.

Getting there: Step one is to fly to Barbados, where you can charter a small plane for the flight to the grass landing area on Palm Island (if it is open at the time of your visit). Otherwise fly on the scheduled-if-erratic service of LIAT to St. Vincent or Grenada and then Union Island, a short swim from Palm (but someone will meet you in a boat for that last link). You can also reach Palm Island by the mailboat service that threads the Grenadine Islands together out of Kingstown, St. Vincent. The best way of all to reach Palm Island, for my money and time, is by charter yacht after you've sailed down the Grenadine Islands from St. Vincent.

PETIT ST. VINCENT RESORT, on its own island of Petit St. Vincent, one of the specks that make up the Grenadine Islands.

Striving for more elegance than at many island retreats, this inn puts you in one of its 22 cottages. If you have a strong preference for being on the beach or up the hillside, say so when you make your reservations and the staff that operates under the direction of Hazen Richardson will do its best to see that you get what you want.

This is a quiet place, with an English tone that includes afternoon tea, a feast in itself from my experience. Although donning your most elegant resort attire has never been part of the plan for Petit St. Vincent (no jacket or tie for men), the comfortably casual atmosphere comes from the understated elegance that sets the tone for the inn. No one takes the "Nobody dresses for dinner" comment literally, as is happening in some Caribbean spots.

Boats and the sea are the main action, with a pier that juts from the sandy shore to provide first footing for nautical types who have been sailing through the islands. Beaches stretch around most of the island's rim, and all are powdery white sand. Water sports such as fishing, scuba diving, and snorkeling are available beachside.

Meals are served in the main house, with its West Indian-style stone walls and the punctuation of ancient cannons and other treasures rescued from the sea.

There are no phones in your room, however you can get room service by raising a flag, the sight of which spurs one of the waiters to action. The necessary furnishings are comfortable and elegant. This is no place for people who must have lots of action, but it is ideal if you want to be coddled while you revive in the Caribbean.

PETIT ST. VINCENT RESORT, Petit St. Vincent, c/o St. Vincent, West Indies. Telephone: 84801. The 22 cottages are open to the breezes and follow a Swedish architect's design. The local bluebitch stone was used for the walls. Most of the furnishings are made from purpleheart wood which used to grow in the islands and now has to be imported. Each villa has its own terrace, private bath, living room, and bedroom with two queen-sized beds. All meals, plus tea, are included in your room rate. The resort is the only place on the island. Children are welcome and baby-sitters can be provided.

Getting there: Count on this being the same adventure that you've read about with other Grenadine Island resorts. Fly to Barbados and then to St. Vincent or Grenada to go on to Union Island (unless you've chartered in Barbados to fly direct to Union). Management will make arrangements for you to be met at the Union Island airstrip and taken by boat for the half-hour crossing to Petit St. Vincent, so you must advise arrival time and method.

COTTON HOUSE HOTEL, on the island of Mustique, one of the Grenadine Islands.

If your idea of an island retreat is a place that is remote, but not impossible to reach, where birds sing, breezes move the fronds of palms, and the beach is just below the porch you can sit on in a comfortable chair, this place is it. The Honorable Colin Tennant conceived the small and perfect island resort in the days when the plantation life thrived in the Caribbean, especially in nearby Barbados where creative Oliver Messel had put decorating flourishes on homes and small hotels. His touch added elegance to the buildings on Mustique.

That was in the late 1960s and for a couple of years, the elegant resort flourished almost as a private club. In 1972, the doors were opened to the general public, at least those who were enterprising and elegant enough to know about the place and charter a plane to get here. By 1976 the Honorable Colin Tennant had wearied of his role as innkeeper; a lease was issued to Guy de la Houssaye, owner of Martinique's Bakoua Hotel.

Enter: A new era for Cotton House. Life is casual, sometimes *very* casual, but life on the 3-mile by 1½-mile speck can still be appealing for non-fussy types who want to share an island with a handful of other folk, many of them Europeans who search for a place in the Caribbean sun.

The main house was built in the best West Indian tradition, with a rectangular stone foundation topped with a second story main room, with balcony, arches, and louvered doors. Cotton House is a place you can easily call home, whether you sit on the verandah to rock and read the day away or head for the beach and sea.

Guest rooms are in several small houses less than 100 yards from the main building, or at the beach cottage at l'Ansecoy Bay about ¼ mile from the hotel and completely self-sufficient, with staff included for the guests who enjoy the two-bedroom house.

The atmosphere is relaxing. Anyone who yearns to recreate the comforts of the plantation days, but is mindful of the changes that have come with the 1970s, can settle in happily. If you're one who wants some action with your sun and sea, there are options for snorkeling, scuba diving, sailing, deep sea fishing, and water-skiing. There is a pool-restaurant-tennis court complex that is the heart of land-based activity during the daytime. The pier at Britannia Bay where you'll find some small shops is your route out to sea.

COTTON HOUSE HOTEL, Mustique Island, St. Vincent, West Indies. Telephone: St. Vincent 83283/83210. Each of the 11 guest rooms in the several houses in the orbit of the main building has twin-bedded facilities, with a balcony, ocean view, and modern bathroom. Oliver Messel's bright and colorful decorator's touch is obvious in the comfortable furnishings. The Beach Cottage at l'Ansecoy Bay sits in a nest of palm trees, seaside. Each of the two bedrooms has twin beds, modern appointments, and private bathroom. Guests share the kitchen, sitting room and open-air dining terrace. A maid is part of your service. Meals can be enjoyed "at home," or at the main house.

Getting there: Plan ahead and be prepared for some delays. The best way to reach Mustique is to charter a small plane from Barbados to fly to the "2,500-foot metalled air-strip" on Mustique. Commerical flights via LIAT connect Barbados to St. Vincent (45 minutes) and then St. Vincent to Mustique (about 10 minutes), but I have never traveled that route without delays. Boats can come into Mustique's Britannia Bay from St. Vincent if you want to make the journey a real excursion.

CRYSTAL SANDS BEACH HOTEL, at the shore on Canouan.
This island is marked for big things, with attention given to it by the central government in St. Vincent and plans for some villa developments. However, when Crystal Sands opened in December 1977, it was the first place for visitors to overnight on the island. Not technically an inn, and not open long enough to earn a time-honored reputation, I mention the place for people who want to go to an island known only to a few boating folk and a handful of other "outsiders."

Canouan is one of the powdery-sand-rimmed small islands that make up the string of the Grenadines, the islands that stretch between St. Vincent and Grenada. When Mr. and Mrs. Phileus De Roche, natives of Canouan, decided to build their place, they realized that most of the visitors would be coming here because it is a simple, quiet spot. What they provide is a comfortable, sparsely furnished, open-air haven for you to huddle into when you want to come in from the sun.

There is a main building which houses the reception area, the dining room and a place for whatever the evening entertainment happens to be, if there is any. The plans for a tennis court and for the mini-golf course hadn't materialized when I visited, but there is still talk of adding them when finances allow and business warrants. The daytime action centers on swimming, sailing, scuba, and snorkeling now.

At the moment, you will find your lodgings are in one of the five villas, each with two double rooms.

CRYSTAL SANDS BEACH HOTEL, c/o Canouan Post Office, Canouan, St. Vincent, W.I. Telephone: not available. The 10 rooms are in five villas, each with two twin-bedded rooms that have private entrances and bathroom facilities. Don't count on luxury, but you will find clean, neat, new accommodations with a sea emphasis.

173

Getting there: Fly first to Barbados and then: 1) Charter to fly for 45 minutes to the airstrip on Canouan; 2) fly to St. Vincent or Grenada on the commercial flight and charter from there (because there is no commercial service to Canouan as I write); or 3) fly to St. Vincent and arrange for passage on the motorboat, M.V. Seimstrand, that chugs its way through the Grenadines with freight and passengers twice weekly. The Seimstrand arrives in Canouan on Mondays and Thursdays, heading south, and departs for St. Vincent, in the north, on Tuesdays and Fridays. (Double check the schedule before you count on it.)

TRINIDAD and TOBAGO

Independent from England since August 1962, the two-island nation is one of the few with money (from oil). The 65 mile by 50 mile island of cosmopolitan Trinidad offers the multi-cultural capital of Port of Spain; plus Maracas Bay Beach along the north shore; a string of satellite small islands (Monos and Gaspar Islands) reached by boat from the city; bird sanctuaries and nature preserves in its swamps and mountain interior and a pitch lake that was used to caulk the ships of Sir Francis Drake. Tobago's 26 miles by 7½ miles are fringed with some of the Caribbean's best beaches. This Robinson Crusoe retreat has remained aloof from the hubbub in the rest of the Caribbean.

Arriving at Piarco Airport on Trinidad is direct on BWIA or Pan American from New York, or BWIA and Eastern with stops out of Miami. Tobago is a 45-minute flight from Piarco Airport on Trinidad & Tobago Air Service, known locally as TTAS. Longer cruises, and those starting from island ports touch Port of Spain, Trinidad.

Star attractions on this intriguing two-island nation include the cosmopolitan life around Port of Spain, Trinidad, where East Indian, West Indian, European, African, and American cultures and customs mix and mingle. Evening activity appeals to the local folk, with pubs, restaurants, discotheques, nightclubs, and special carnival activities just before the start of Lent. Tobago is a quiet island with the beach-and-sun life. There's history in the hills, fort ruins that have been restored at Scarborough and Plymouth, fishing off the shores and the local fishermen to entertain with their catch at the sunset hours.

Action options when you stay in Trinidad, can include a day excursion by boat (check Holiday Inn's activities desk) to a Monos Island beach, spend a day (with hotel-packed picnic and waiting driver) at Maracas Bay; a walk through the Asa Wright Sanctuary, an hour's drive into the mountains; a tour of the island's hinterland (figure about $10 per person for 4 hours); see-ing a traditional spice and fruit market at Beetham Highway, out-side Port of Spain; watching cricket matches and other sports (horse racing) around the Queen's Park Savanah; and looking at an intriguing array of architecture in the Victorian buildings around Savannah and speckled in Port of Spain.

On Tobago, small but elegant resort nightlife is the most usual fare for tourists with dancing by starlight to steel bands, perhaps some local entertainment, and quiet evenings around the pool or at a beach barbecue with hotel guests. At Buccoo Village, near most resorts, there's an island show given by the village folk on a regualr schedule. Spectacular Buccoo Reef, a 2-hour boat excursion offshore, was plucked to average status before ecologists established rules, but it's still worth a visit. The small boat tour out of Buccoo Village, arranged through your hotel, costs about $10.

Best beaches on Trinidad are remote spots, an excursion from most places visitors are likely to be, but if you are in the Port of Spain area, a boat ride to the islands, a drive to the beaches at Chagaramus or a day-with-picnic over the mountains to the long strand at Maracas Bay are worth the effort. Tobago is the beach island. You will find sandy ribbons near most hotels and inns, but there are lovely long strands that you can share with a few fishermen or a sea bird or two. With a rental car, you will be able to find your haven.

For further information in New York, contact the Trinidad & Tobago Tourist Board, 400 Madison Avenue, New York, New York 10017. Telephone: (212) 838-7750. The Trinidad and Tobago Tourist Board has offices on the second floor at 56 Frederick Street, Port of Spain, Trinidad, West Indies. (25¢ postage per half-ounce airmail.)

ARNOS VALE, on its own cove, amidst a 400-acre estate, northeast of the village of Plymouth.

This place has received plaudits, and manager Ean Mackay seems to like to pile them all one on top of the other, regardless of when the comments were made. Thus, praise in guidebooks and the prestige of having been a member of the Relais de Campagne at some time in its history are both noted in current brochures in spite of the fact that the guidebook comment comes from an obsolete edition, the Relais honor was withdrawn and there have been changes in management, customs, and service.

None of that is crucial, however, unless you come here expecting white-glove treatment and French cuisine. Neither of those things, nor a lot of other colonial-style luxuries are available here. But what is available is plenty good enough for most of us, and makes the place the ideal Tobagonian base for the bird-watching and flora/fauna tours operated by Questers Tours & Travel.

First, the setting: Over the 20 years that I have known this place, the foliage has had to be controlled by brutal pruning, but the results are perfect. Tropical growth spills over and around the buildings, even covering the newest part that is down by the beach. There's a comfortable feeling of permanence that doesn't come with the newly built inns.

The main house at the top of the hill is where you will find the reception rooms and the chintz-covered chairs and couches that lend such a comfortable air to the place. There's an open-air patio, a much-talked about Murano glass chandelier and a grand piano that is supposed to have been played in the Paris Exhibition of 1851, plus the dining room that now features island cuisine, and serves it well.

The Sunday Creole Buffet served near the beach is island famous. Guests from other hotels join residents (and your colleagues who have been smart enough to book a room here) for the feast.

The nooks and crannies pounded into the black rocks at the east end of the beach are perfect for wallowing in a sea wash, when you tire of the ideal swimming around the bay. There is a tennis court for more strenuous exercise, a pool, and the opportunity to go horsebacking riding if you state your wishes at the front desk.

ARNOS VALE, Plymouth, Box 208, Scarborough, Tobago, West Indies. Telephone: Tobago 639-2881/2. The 25 rooms and 3 suites are draped from hilltop to shoreline, with the most interesting rooms being in the original hotel at the top of the hill. This is where you will find the suites. Both Coral and Dolphin

Cottages have hilltop views; Jacamar Suite is beachside. There are 15 rooms in and around the main house, and 8 more at the second level of the 2-story building down by the beach where the daytime restaurant is located.

Getting there: Unless you have hopped onto one of the nonstop flights to Tobago, you will have to change planes at Trinidad's Piarco Airport for the half-hour flight to the smaller island. Once on Tobago, a taxi will take you for the 45-minute ride along the north coast, through the village of Plymouth to the Arnos Vale Estate.

MOUNT ST. BENEDICT GUEST HOUSE, Tunapuna, Trinidad, W.I.

Anyone braced for cosmopolitan, multi-faceted, bustling Port of Spain will be pleasantly surprised by the peace and quiet of this mountain inn. It stands on the grounds of a Benedictine Monastery, about half an hour's drive into the mountains from the Piarco Airport.

The Abbey of Mount St. Benedict celebrated its Diamond Jubilee in 1972. Monks fleeing oppression in Brazil came to Trinidad to establish a retreat in 1911 and, at the invitation of an elderly gentleman of Spanish descent, Dom Mayuel, made the trip along Eastern Main Road to the Village of St. John where the road came to an end. *"After a stiff climb, a small hut was reached, occupied by an East Indian named Kisto Barcoa, factotum of the estate. The hut measured some 15 feet by 9 feet and was built of mud. It had a thatched roof and the interior was divided into two small compartments. Beneath the floor there were cocoa drying trays. The view took the Abbot by storm and conquered him. Dom Mayuel was impressed by the solitude and solemn stillness of the place. He was enchanted by its natural beauty and refreshed by the coolness of the water."*

The hilltop is still tranquil today, but the road that slithers up from Tunapuna is much better than the steep climb by foot made by Dom Mayuel long ago. At the top is a large church, dwellings, several schools, a small shop, and the Guest House, all built by the monks over the past 60 years.

The Guest House, now operated under the auspices of the Christian Council of Churches, is a short walk below the church, but within earshot of the bells. The view from the hilltop and from the rooms in the Guest House is still as impressive as ever. The stillness and natural beauty are still there, and so is a pleasant staff, working under the experienced eye of Ms. Elaine Harris.

Food, served on the covered porch facing the small garden, is simple and substantial. There is a pool a short way down the hill. It is part of the school facilities but may sometimes be used by guests.

MOUNT ST. BENEDICT GUEST HOUSE, Tunapuna, Trinidad, West Indies. Telephone: not available. The 11 rooms are simple, clean, and neat. All have sinks, some have private baths. Each room is different, as you would expect in a private house. Two rooms at the front overlook plains and cane fields below. Walking and reading are the main activities. This is a place to rest.

Getting there: A taxi from Trinidad's Piarco Airport takes about half an hour and costs $14TT each way. A bus runs from the Mount into Tunapuna to connect with the public bus which makes several stops enroute to Port of Spain. You'll need a rental car if you want to be mobile.

UNITED STATES VIRGIN ISLANDS

The triumvirate of U.S. Virgins (St. Croix, St. Thomas, and St. John) is a special duty-free port, in spite of status as a territory under the United States flag. Still benefitting from a decree that was part of the transfer from the Danes in 1917, the towns of Charlotte Amalie (U.S.V.I. capital on St. Thomas) and Christiansted and Frederiksted on St. Croix hold some of the world's luxuries at free port prices.

About 40 miles east of Puerto Rico, the three islands are home for about 100,000 people, with major portions on the 13 miles by 3 miles of St. Thomas and the 28 miles by 7 miles of St. Croix. Most of the 7 miles by 5 miles of St. John are the 29th U.S. National Park, one of the few official campgrounds in the Caribbean.

Arriving is easy by air to St. Croix direct from New York, Miami, and Puerto Rico and to St. Thomas from Puerto Rico and St. Croix (until the airport extensions are completed and super jets can land here). St. John has no airport. It is reached by boat or sea plane from St. Thomas.

Cruise lines have made St. Thomas the Caribbean's number one port, lured by the free port status that allows visitors $200 worth of duty-free goods and one gallon of liquor. (All other Caribbean places have the usual $100 and one bottle allotment.) Some cruises stop at Frederiksted, St. Croix, and the locally based Antilles Air Boats sea plane service flits between the United States Virgin Islands and the neighboring British Virgins on regular schedules.

Star attractions for this trio are the expected lures of the Caribbean (sun, sand, sea) with liberal portions of 20th century modern trappings (good roads, telex and telephone communication with the United States and the world, modern facilities and name brand stores including Woolworths, Grand Union and their ilk). Watersports are important enough to have their own division within the local Department of Commerce and the nightlife options offer everything but gambling. St. John's top attractions are natural—beaches, forts, and flora.

Action options are sea-oriented during the day, with top facilities for scuba diving for beginners and experts, several charter boat firms with luxury yachts and day sailors for exploring nearby coves, snorkeling and the option for looking at the underwater life without getting wet at the innovative Coral World off Coki Point on the east end of St. Thomas. Christiansted, the main town on St. Croix, is a National Monument which means that most of its Danish West Indian buildings have been restored and refurbished to look much as they might have in the 1700s. Buck Island is an offshore goal.

Best beaches are on St. John, all around the island, but with facilities at the campgrounds, at Maho Bay Camps and at luxury Caneel Bay. St. Thomas beaches are out of town, along Lindberg Bay near the airport, and Morningstar Beach and the southcoast stretching east, as well as at Magens Bay and other north shore coves. St. Croix has beaches at some of the coves along its north shore, along the west coast north and south of Frederiksted, and at some hotels in the Christiansted area, but the best beaches are at the east end, near Jack's Bay and beyond Cramer Park's public beach, and at Buck Island.

For further information, the main office in the U.S. is the Virgin Islands Information Center, 10 Rockefeller Plaza, New York, New York 10020. Telephone: (212) 582-4520. On location, there are tourist offices at the waterfront in Christiansted, St. Croix, U.S.V.I. as well as at the waterfront and near the cruise ship dock at Charlotte Amalie, St. Thomas, U.S.V.I. Address correspondance to the Visitors' Bureau, Christiansted, St. Croix, U.S.V.I. or to the Visitors' Bureau, Box 1692, Charlotte Amalie, St. Thomas, U.S.V.I.

ANCHOR INN, in the heart of Christiansted, St. Croix, U.S.V.I.

You have to get inside to appreciate this inn. It's hard to see from the small courtyard that opens into the hotel's entrance, just off King Street, the main island-to-waterside thoroughfare of Christiansted.

Owned and supervised by Lon Southerland, the Anchor Inn has recently been given a new lease on life. The inn began as the Old Quarter Hotel, tucked into an already crowded area, in the late 1960s. It was designed to rise from a small base, on several balconied levels, giving the feeling of the cozy privacy you might find in a Mediterranean village. The plan works, but don't count on a spectacular view from every room.

The restaurant is reached through the small entrance into the open courtyard and up a stone stairway. It is pure Sidney Greenstreet—swinging wicker chairs, plenty of air, light, and plants, even though the view is limited by surrounding buildings. Food and drink are served in these congenial surroundings, not only to hotel guests but to others smart enough to ferret out this place. San Francisco sets the tone.

Within a few steps from this island hideaway are all the assets of a U.S. National Historic Site. Most of the town of Christiansted, headquarters of the Danish West Indies government prior to the purchase of the islands by the United States in 1917, dates from the 18th century, when it was a center of Caribbean trade and commerce.

The National Park Service operates walking tours through and around the 17th century Fort Christiansvaern, the Danish Post Office, the Steeple Building with its small museum, and sometimes into the Government Buildings.

Even if you don't remember that Christiansted is where young Alexander Hamilton worked in the family hardware store after coming from his birthplace on nearby Nevis to stay with relatives, you will enjoy the combination of 18th and 20th century atmospheres. Luxury import stores and a host of island boutiques and restaurants, nestled into the restored buildings. A full range of water sports—sailing, snorkeling, scuba diving, and Buck Island boat trips—are right outside the Anchor Inn's back door if you follow the footpath that leads along the waterfront from the small pool.

ANCHOR INN, 58 King Street, Christiansted, St. Croix, U.S.V.I. Telephone: (809) 773-4000. The 30 rooms are convenient. Count on a modern room with air conditioning and a small refrigerator. If you are lucky you will have room 3S which has one of the town's best harbor views. But other rooms, smaller and with minimal views, still provide all comforts. There is no beach, only a small pool for dunking.

Getting there: Taxi from the mid-island airport will take about 20 minutes. Make arrangements in advance for a taxi for your return flight, whether you go from the big airport, or fly the seaplane service on Antilles Airboats, just a short walk away.

CANE BAY PLANTATION, King's Hill, St. Croix, U.S.V.I.

The Plantation has been here for years; parts of it, in fact, for more than 200 years, when the core was first built by a Dane as a second home in the then-Danish Virgin Islands. Always a getaway place, the property never had the kind of formal "Great House" that has been graciously restored elsewhere. Cane Bay Plantation has always been an informal Shangri-La on the north coast of St. Croix.

When I first learned about it, some 20 years ago, it was owned by a couple from New England. They were among the pioneers of an intrepid band of northerners fleeing to the warmth of the Caribbean. Guests then stayed in the slave quarters, small rectangular cottages scattered behind the main building.

Today, under genial owner/operators Sally and Charles Goit, the slave quarters, much refurbished but intact, are still in use. Most guests, however, stay in the newer part, a two-story building near the sea. Rooms are modern, with no phones. The sole contact with the outside world is the *New York Times.* There's one well-shared copy for the inn.

Renowned for its house party atmosphere, Cane Bay's 40 guests take their cue from their sometimes boisterous, always delightful ex-Madison Avenue, host, and the calming influence of his capable wife.

The food's a feature, a special hobby of the Goits who have kept a loyal and pleasant staff with them for most of the years since Charles acquired the property in 1963. Specialties in the menu are international. Each night there is something different, perhaps Armenian lemon soup, Italian lasagna, Chinese butterfly shrimp, French duckling, or New England corned beef and cabbage. The Sunday buffet, a brunch, draws residents and hotel guests from the rest of the island for a pleasant, island outing.

You are definitely on your own—even to taking care of your tally for beverages when the bartender is not on duty—and you can do exactly what you please as long as it doesn't rock the boat for other guests. The Plantation is more like a friendly home than a hotel.

CANE BAY PLANTATION, P.O. Box G, King's Hill Station, St. Croix, U.S.V.I. 00858. Telephone: (809) 778-0410. Most of the twin-bedded hotel rooms are in a two-story building facing the sea. A few are in two converted slave quarter cottages. Total house count is 40 guests. The inn is on the north coast of St. Croix, about a 25-minute drive along a good road to the Fountain Valley Golf Course (a 10-minute drive on the rugged back road). Scuba and snorkeling are excellent off the hotel's beach, a good one. There is also a small pool. Ask about special golf and scuba packages and other week-long vacation plans.

Getting there: Fly to St. Croix for the taxi ride across the island to the north coast (about half an hour). Rental cars are advisable for touring but not necessary for a beach and lounging holiday.

SPRAT HALL, a few miles up the west coast, north of Frederiksted.
If island history and traditions intrigue you, you'll find the hospitality offered by Jim and Joyce Hurd perfect for your island holiday. Not only are they related to one of the "big five" Cruzan families—the families that owned most of the land at the turn of the century—but they also have made the island their home through thick and thin, running their venerable inn which is also their home. Some of the flock of Hurd children have flown their island nest, but all come home to roost frequently as do many of the people who have found this spot as a vacation home.

The main house is a typical Cruzan plantation home, and

most of the furnishings are family heirlooms that have seen a lot of use through the centuries. The furniture in your room will probably include a four-poster bed, but will certainly include a lot of Victoriana.

This is an inn for outdoors folk. The Hurds' own ponies are available for you to ride, and no one can contest Jim Hurd's expert fishing sense. He and his various fishing boats have been going out to bring in the supper for as long as I have known the family, and that covers some 20 years.

Do not count on fancy, modern conveniences. All the necessaries are here, but the house maintains its traditional atmosphere and is not the place to go if you demand sleek modernities.

In addition to the porch and pool at the main house, there is a nice beachhouse down the path and across the road at the shore. The main house is on a rise (as was the custom, to take advantage of the breezes), overlooking the sea which you can see if the shrubs have been cut.

SPRAT HALL, Box 695, Frederiksted, St. Croix, U.S. Virgin Islands. Telephone: (809) 772-0305. Of the 25 rooms, 22 have air-conditioners. There are some newer rooms, added in the last 10 years, but the most interesting accommodations (and the best value) are those in the old house.

Getting there: Fly to St. Croix and take a taxi to Frederiksted and up the west coast. The ride will take about half an hour.

HARBOR VIEW, on a hillside in Charlotte Amalie, St. Thomas, U.S.V.I.

Several years ago Arlene Lockwood scoured small shops in downtown New York for the right kind of copper kettles to fit the new decor at Harbor View. Not long after that, with the help of colleague Leonore Wolfe, the Mediterranean-style menu was ready. The new look was ushered in and the transformation from old house to chic island inn was complete.

The house had been standing for decades—but not too securely. As the new owners soon found out, termites and time had taken their toll. The place needed (and got) a complete overhaul.

Ricky Challifoux, one of the flamboyant island personalities of 20 years ago, was the first to open this place as a small guest house. The Agells, a Scandinavian couple, then took over the long-term lease and put their considerable building and decorating talents to use to create a restoration of the former Danish West Indian architecture, food, and decor.

And then came another change. Arlene Lockwood set up island residence, commuting at first between New York and St. Thomas, and putting her individual stamp on the 10 rooms of the house. Each is now furnished with wicker and colorful fabric. It's simple, but comfortable.

My favorite spot—and a must for every visit to St. Thomas—is the terrace at twilight and even later. Island-renowned for its interesting menu and near-perfect service, with fine tableware and elegant crystal, Harbor View is tops for dining out. Reservations are essential, and so is arriving early, so that you can sit in the comfortable terrace lounges overlooking the lights and harbor of Charlotte Amalie.

The location is not ideal, although the view is. The inn is in an area of the town of St. Thomas where twenty years of rapid growth have filled every square inch with buildings, and most buildings with too many people. The nearby houses are far from elegant; the road leading from the downtown marketplace twists and convolutes, through narrow, thronged streets, to climb to this oasis. Taxis take you here (it's only about five minutes from downtown) or you can drive yourself, parking just outside the front door.

Lingering by the pool, which was added a few seasons ago in a former garden just below the house, is perfect during the daytime. Luncheon is sometimes served poolside, usually by reservation or on weekends.

HARBOR VIEW, Box 1974, Charlotte Amalie, St. Thomas, U.S.V.I. Telephone: (809) 774-2651. The 10 rooms are all shapes and sizes, each with an air conditioning unit. They may or may not have views. Appointments are colorful, clean, and pleasant, not lavish. The Harbor View terrace and poolside are convening areas. The restaurant draws a large evening crowd. Life is casual here.

Getting there: From the airport, take a taxi into town and up the hill, the ride will take about 15 minutes.

HOTEL 1829, on Government Hill in Charlotte Amalie, St. Thomas, U.S.V.I.

About three minutes from Government House with its American and Virgin Islands flags flying, the inn perches at a prominent part of the town. A stroll down the steps or following the road down Government Hill into the hundreds of Charlotte Amalie shops takes no more than five minutes.

Hotel 1829 had a special personality about 20 years ago when former owner Mrs. Maguire would hold court on the terrace before or after dinner provided by Chef Thomas. The place still is special but St. Thomas has changed a lot, and so has Hotel 1829. The inn still looks the same. It has to. It is part of a National Historic Site.

Inside, however, things are more comfortable than they once were. The dining rooms, both inside and on the terrace, are colorful, with the feeling of a French bistro. Island residents often come up for the backgammon tournaments planned by the inn's owner, Baron Vernon A. Ball, a world backgammon champion.

The casual, comfortable bar has balast brick walls, sandblasted into view during the most recent renovations. The homey atmosphere is helped along by Billy, the bartender who has been here long enough to recognize you when you return. A popular place to pause (perhaps for lunch) when you're downtown in Charlotte Amalie, Hotel 1829 has its devoted coterie of repeat visitors.

The beach is a 10-minute drive from the inn, but there's a small pool on the premises, through the courtyard and up the cement steps, amidst a cascade of colorful bougainvillea.

HOTEL 1892, Kongensgaad 30, Box 1579, Charlotte Amalie, St. Thomas, U.S.V.I. Telephone: (809) 774-1829. A lot of variety is included among the 19 rooms. The ones on the front of the house get the view (and the noise), plus terraces. All rooms have private baths, which may mean that the room is small. After all, there's only so much space and private bathrooms were not part of the plans when the original house was built. The restaurant emphasizes European cuisine, in bistro surroundings. Sauna, pool, and backgammon for diversion.

Getting there: About a 15-minute drive from the airport; only 10 minutes if you come in on seaplane service via Antilles Air Boats to the Charlotte Amalie waterfront.

MAFOLIE, nestled into the mountainside overlooking the harbor of Charlotte Amalie.

Most people come to Mafolie for meals, but the few who find a room here are in for a special treat. After the dining and dancing crowd has wound back down the mountain to their overnight nests, the place is peaceful, quiet and serene. The view from here is spectacular. You can wake with the sunrise, as it comes up over the hills shedding the first light on the harbor and igniting its daily activity.

Mafolie was originally built as an island home, and it still has that homey feeling. There's a small pool with a sundeck to give guests a place for a quick dip, but most visitors take their rental cars off to some beach for a day in the Caribbean Sea. For those who make reservations for one of the 23 rooms, there's an inner circle of hospitality.

Your breakfast is served on the dining terrace that lights up at night for the popular buffet or steak-and-fish dinners.

The zigzagging road route that puts you 800 feet above Charlotte Amalie is the same route that leads on up and over the main St. Thomian mountain range to Magen's Bay. The inn provides free transportation daily to the beach and management will arrange for sailing and fishing expeditions, as well as assist with your plans for a day at St. John or perhaps a quick flight to neighboring St. Croix for a day tour.

MAFOLIE, Box 1528, St. Thomas, U.S. Virgin Islands. Telephone: (809) 774-2790. The 23 rooms come in all shapes and sizes. After the first ones were built, others were built as time, money, and ingenuity permitted. Twenty of the rooms are air-conditioned; a couple of them have views. Most rooms are small, but private bath is one convenience you can count on.

Getting there: Fly to St. Thomas from either Puerto Rico or St. Croix (until the airport lengthening is finished on big planes from U.S. cities, when you will be able to fly nonstop direct. And that's expected to be sometime in 1979.) From the airport, take a taxi for the 20-minute ride into town and up into the hills behind Charlotte Amalie.

GALLEON HOUSE, on Government Hill, a three-minute walk up from the Post Office and Main Street, Charlotte Amalie, St. Thomas.

In the early 50s, when Ben and Ginny Yates opened Galleon House, they used to keep a bottle of champagne in the refrigerator. It was served, with ceremony, at breakfast, to the first guest who came down the stone steps in the breakfast area and didn't say, "My God, those roosters!"

The roosters seldom crow in Charlotte Amalie anymore. The town is now too cosmopolitan, and the owners of the guest house have changed several times. Larry Evans fled from northern winters at the Bird and Bottle Inn in Garrison, New York, to become the fourth and present owner.

The inn still looks the same from the outside as it did when I first saw it, except for some severe pruning and plucking of the overgrown garden just inside the fence. That effort has helped to open up the place a lot. There's also the addition of private bath with the rooms (no such luxury existed in the early days) and sprucing up of the overnight accommodations, as well as the gathering areas. The piano still serves as magnet in the evenings, and the deck that hangs over the hubbub of Charlotte Amalie provides a spectacular view at sunset and an ideal spot to spend a few hours daydreaming.

Dining has always been comfortably casual, with several small tables on an open deck, and dinners sometimes served buffet style from a wide wood shelf that runs along the stone wall of the oldest part of the house.

On my most recent visit, there were rumors of plans for building a small pool, but that will take some doing since the space for it will have to be created out of thin air and firm footing. The nearest beaches are at Lindberg Bay or the Morningstar area, and both are a ten-minute drive from town. You can, however, walk to most of the in-town restaurants.

GALLEON HOUSE, Box 1189, St. Thomas, U.S.V.I. 0081. Telephone (809) 774-1445. The 15 rooms (10 of them air-conditioned) are scattered around the house and a couple of appended buildings that are incorporated into the maze that now comprises the small inn. All rooms have private bath, wall-to-wall carpeting, and are comfortable, though varied in size and view.

Getting there: Galleon House is a short walk from the waterfront, up the hill past the post office, and next door to Hotel 1829. Take a taxi for the ten-minute ride from the St. Thomas Airport.

VILLA OLGA, through Frenchtown, at the harborside on the fringes of downtown Charlotte Amalie, St. Thomas, U.S.V.I.

Everyone loves to talk about Villa Olga having been the Russian Consulate. That was in the 1800s, hence the name. But don't get the idea that this inn is big and pretentious. It is small and quite simple—a typical West Indian wooden house that has seen a lot of history (and some hard times). New management and ownership in late 1977 resulted in a general refurbishing, which it certainly needed. The physical looks and location are typical island-casual, and fun.

The somewhat seedy area you drive through to get to the inn, off the main waterfront road through town, is the old-time residential area for early St. Thomian settlers coming from St. Barths. Since St. Barthélemy is French, the neighborhood's nickname is Frenchtown. Nestling among the shacks and simple dwellings are a couple of good restaurants and some charter boat firms.

Underwater life is the focus for the "new" Villa Olga. The garden area that stretches from the front porch to the sea is still used for dining as is the porch, but underwater instructors also make this place their hub, with each expert taking guests out for a dive-a-day (or a couple of dives depending on the depth and location).

Something to think about when planning to stay here (in addition to the nautical atmosphere) is the fact that the Antilles Air Boats seaplanes sweep through the narrow gut on their several daily trips in and out of St. Thomas. While they are fascinating to watch, they are also noisy.

There is a salt water pool and, if you don't mind swimming in the harbor, a sea-lined shore. Heading to better beaches will probably be the route you'll take for Caribbean Sea swimming. Boats dock just offshore so there is always plenty to look at.

VILLA OLGA, Box 4976, Charlotte Amalie, St. Thomas, U.S.V.I. Telephone: (809) 774-1376. Of the 18 rooms, only one was air-conditioned in the "old" days, but the new management, with their paint-and-scrub efforts, are air conditioning others. Accommodations are simple, with rooms of varied size and location in the main house and neighboring outbuildings.

Getting there: About 10 minutes by taxi from St. Thomas Airport. Within walking distance of the shops in town, if you don't mind the saunter through Frenchtown. Most people don't.

MAGENS POINT HOTEL, on the north coast, overlooking the Caribbean with a few of the British Virgin Islands on the horizon.

Perched on the hillside on the verdant north coast, the inn opened almost ten years ago as Indies House. For a while, the previous management attempted to operate a tropical zoo on the premises, in addition to the gardens, pool, and popular "Lobster Pot" restaurant.

The wiggly road to get here, whether you drive up and over the mountain from Charlotte Amalie and the airport, or take the east end road around from town to the north coast, leads through some rural areas of St. Thomas. You'll pass St. Thomas Dairies and most of the island's farms, many of them operated by French settlers originally from the island of St. Barths.

The avocado green buildings that hold most of the rooms are at the highest point of the complex, but are connected to the pool and restaurant area with sidewalks that slant (no steps) for easy strolling. In late 1976, when Lon Southerland from St. Croix's Anchor Inn led a group in buying the place, there was a lot of work to do to get things back in shape. The zoo has gone, the name has changed to Magens Point Hotel, and the entire property has undergone a scrub and polish routine. New poolside lounge chairs and a gradual refurbishing of all the bedrooms have helped to create the new atmosphere.

For those who want the beach, the inn provides free transportation down the hill to the famous strand of sand at Magens Bay. A rental car will give you more mobility if you want to travel around the island to sample other seaside spots.

MAGENS POINT HOTEL, Magens Bay Road, St. Thomas, United States Virgin Islands. Telephone: (809) 774-8552. The 30 rooms are all alike, with carpeted floor, modern bath and efficiency units in the rooms, and balconies with a view over the Caribbean and neighboring islands. There are two double beds in most rooms.

Getting there: If you rent a car at the airport to drive up, allow about 20 minutes and count on getting lost unless you keep looking for the "Lobster Pot" restaurant signs that point the way at every possible turning point. The general route is to drive through Charlotte Amalie, turning left just after the fort. Keep on that road to the end, turn left and wiggle and wind up the mountain, over the pass and down the other side. The hotel is clearly marked. Taxis also make the run from the airport.